AVKO Sequential Spelling 3 for Home Study Learning

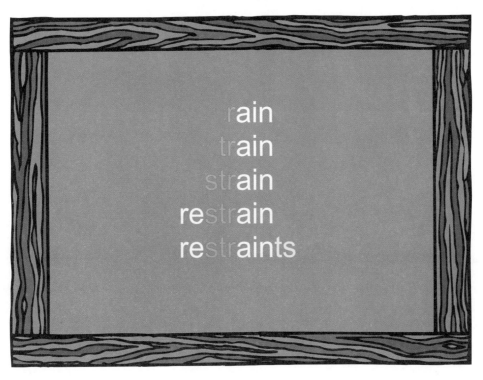

rain
train
strain
restrain
restraints

by

Don McCabe
Research Director
AVKO Educational Research Foundation

Dedication

This book is dedicated to:
All the members of the AVKO Educational Research Foundation,
but especially to the memory of one of its first members,

Mary Clair Scott
without whose work and devotion to the cause of literacy,
the AVKO Foundation might never have gotten off the ground,

Betty June Szilagyi
who was my first and by far my most important teacher,

Devorah Wolf
without whose encouragement and commitment
to the ideals of AVKO
this edition would not be possible,

Ann, Robert, and Linda McCabe
all of whom have sacrificed much of their time and energy
helping AVKO grow
as well as all those friends and relatives
who have been a source of encouragement.

May this book help you to help others improve their abilities to read and write.

1 2 3 4 5 6 7 8 9 10 11 Printing   Year 03 93 92 89 87 85 83 81 79 76 74

Publisher's Cataloging in Publication Data
McCabe, Donald J.
1. Spelling—Miscellanea 2. Reading—Miscellanea 3. Curriculum—Miscellanea 4. Literacy.
Library of Congress Subject Headings: Spelling, Reading, Curriculum
Library of Congress Classification Number: LB1050.2F79
Library of Congress Card Number: To be determined
Dewey Decimal Classification Number 428.4
ISBN: 1-56400-963-7

AVKO Educational Research Foundation, Inc.
3084 W. Willard Road
Clio, MI 48420
Telephone: (810) 686-9283 FAX (810) 686-1101
Websites: www.avko.org and www.spelling.org Email: info@avko.org

The Basic Concepts of Teaching Spelling by Word Families

You may have used the concept of rhyming words that have the same letter endings to help your students learn to read. For example, you may have introduced the word *at*, then also shared *cat*, *bat*, *sat*, and maybe even *scat*. Unfortunately, you have never had any source book for finding all the rhyming words with the same spelling patterns. [NOTE: In the latest academic jargon word families are now called "rimes." The consonants, consonant blends, and digraphs that precede the word family (or rime) are now called onsets. Use whatever term you wish with your students. In this book, I generally use the terms *base* or *word family* rather than the new jargon word "rime."]

The Patterns of English Spelling (formerly *Word Families Plus*) is now available to be used as a source book so that you can teach any word family. This is not just a simple collection of word lists. This book consists of complete patterns to help your students (and quite often parents and teachers!) see patterns that exist and to lock in on those patterns with their "computer" brains. For example, I believe that if you can teach your students (or anyone) the word *at*, you can also teach them:

bat	bats	batted	batting		
cat	cats				
scat	scats				
flat	flats	flatted	flatting		
pat	pats	patted	patting		
spat	spats				
mat	mats	matted	matting		
rat	rats	ratted	ratting		
batter	batters	battered	battering	battery	batteries
flatter	flatters	flattered	flattering	flattery	
matter	matters	mattered	mattering		
battle	battles	battled	battling		
cattle					
rattle	rattles	rattled	rattling		

OR, for a more sophisticated example, from the word **act** you can build:

act	acts	acted	acting	active	action
fact	facts				
tract	tracts				traction
attract	attracts	attracted	attracting	attractive	attraction
distract	distracts	distracted	distracting		distraction
extract	extracts	extracted	extracting	extractive	extraction
subtract	subtracts	subtracted	subtracting		subtraction
contract	contracts	contracted	contracting		contraction

Perhaps the most important difference between the traditional approach to spelling and the AVKO (**A**udio-**V**isual-**K**inesthetic-**O**ral) approach is that we use tests as a

learning device and **not** as a method of **evaluation**. I believe that the natural method of learning is learning from mistakes, and that is why I want children to correct their own mistakes **when** they make them—so they can learn from them.

We developed the *AVKO Sequential Spelling Tests* to utilize the word family approach sequentially and to apply the very simple techniques of having students correct their own mistakes **when** they make them—not hours, days, or even weeks later.

Use a Dry Erase Board or Something Similar to Give AVKO Sequential Spelling Tests

---

The First Day

On your first day of using Sequential Spelling 3, share with your students:

I have some good news and some bad news. First the bad news. Today and every day until we finish this book, we are going to have a spelling test. The good news is that each one of you will correct your own paper. But before we start, I want each of you to take out a sheet of paper and put your name on it. Did you spell your name correctly? Good. That's my first test. My next test is like a doctor's test. It's not for a grade so don't worry about it. Okay? Now write the following sentence:

> **My best friend is going through a terrible depression.**

If any of your students shows signs of struggling with the sentence, just ask them to try to spell the word **depression** only. If they still find it difficult to put down anything, ask them to just put down—in any order—some of the letters that might be in the word **depression**.

Now collect their papers.

On the 4th day, you will be able to demonstrate that your students who couldn't spell **depression** on the first day were able to correctly spell it without ever having seen or studied the word. And remember that according to Harry Greene's *The New Iowa Spelling Scale* (1954) only 4% of all public school 3rd graders can be expected to spell the word **session** and just 58% of all public school 8th graders can spell the word **session**! We will expect that you will point that out to your students on the 5th day.

If your students have their own copy of the *AVKO Student Response Book for Sequential Spelling*, have them open their books to page 3. Note the location of Day 1. It is in the *middle* column of page 3. Day 2 is in the middle column on page 5. Day 3 is in the middle column on page 7. Day 4 is in the middle column on page 9, and so forth. Please note the AVKO motto on the bottom of these pages:

Mistakes are Opportunities to Learn

The reason for this arrangement is to prevent students from copying the base word that they had the day before and then just adding the -s, -ed, or -ing ending as the case may be. Just as students don't learn by copying from others, they don't learn by copying from themselves.

If your students don't have a Student Response Book, have them use a notebook with single sheets of paper. Use one sheet for each day's spelling lesson."

● *In the column marked 1st day/Lesson 1, please write the word "**gas**" as in: "We have a **gas** furnace. **gas**.*

After your students have attempted writing **gas**, ask them what the first letter of **gas** is. Hopefully they will shout out, "G!" Now, you write on the dry erase board (or something similar) just the letter "g." Now ask what the last two letters of **gas** are. Again, they might shout out, "A-S!" If anyone shouts out A-S-S, tell him it was an intelligent misspelling. You would think it would be spelled gass just like glass, mass, and pass. But the words gas and alas are the two exceptions to this word family.

On the dry erase board you now show the -as. (It really doesn't matter what color you use for the A and the S. I personally like to use green for the word family patterns to contrast later on with the black *beginning letters.*)

Depending upon the age of your students and their attitudes, you may try to get them to spell aloud the word with you (the oral channel) as they trace over their corrected spelling (the kinesthetic channel).

● Then give the second word, **gasoline** as in: *How many gallons of* **gasoline** *did you buy?* **gasoline**.

After your students have attempted the word **gasoline**, you write the beginning g in black, the **as** in green and then the **o** in red, and the **line** in blue. Some students may ask why the "leen" sound in gasoline isn't spelled -leen or -lean. You might want to tell them that they asked a really good question for which there isn't any really good answer. All we can say is that big words tend to follow different phonic patterns because big words generally have come into our language from other languages, and in most other languages the sound "EE" is spelled with the letter *i*. Other examples are p*i*zza, macaron*i*, mar*i*ne, and pet*i*te.

● *The third word is* **alas**. **Alas**, *nothing is as simple as it seems.* **alas**.

Alas is a strange homophone. Its homophonic twin is the next pair of words.

● *The fourth word is* **a lass**. *A girl is often referred to as* **a lass**, *especially in Scotland.*

As you go through the procedure with lass, we recommend that you work through the words backwards! In other words, this time ask what the last three letters are and then show –ass written in green. Then ask what letter comes before the sound of "ass." Show the lass and ask if they can hear the sound lass in glass (number 5) and lass in class (number 6). Continue through the words for this lesson using this procedure.

---

1. Say the word. Use it in a sentence. Say the word again.

2. Write the ending sound (either –as, -ass, -es, or -ess in green.

3. Write the beginning sounds in black in front of the ending letters to make the word.

4. Have your students check their spelling and if necessary correct it.

5. Go to the next word.

The fifth word for today is **glass**. *Will someone get me a glass of water please?* **glass**.

The sixth word for today is **class**. *When will this* **class** *be over?*

7. **grass** *The* **grass** *is always greener over the septic tank.* **grass**

8. **pass** *I would like to get a free* **pass** *to the circus.* **pass**

9. **trespass** *Don't you dare* **trespass** *onto my property.* **trespass**

10. **surpass** *I hope all of you will* **surpass** *my previous class.* **surpass**

11. **mass** *Some of my best friends go to* **mass** *every Sunday.* **mass**

12. ** **bass** *The first fish I ever caught was a large mouth* **bass**. **bass**

13. **brass** *There are times in which I really enjoy a big* **brass** *band.* **brass**

14. **yes** *Just answer the question* **yes** *or no.* **yes**

15. **mess** *The little kids left the house in a mess.* **mess**

16. **guess** *Can you* **guess** *who got blamed for it.* **guess**

17. **dress** *My mother bought herself a* **dress** *for Mother's Day.* **dress**

18. **undress** *Most people* **undress** *before they go to bed.* **undress**

19. **process** *I hope the government will* **process** *our tax refund soon.* **process**

20. **success** *The surprise party was a great* **success**. **success**

21. **bless** *The couple asked the priest to* **bless** *their marriage.* **bless**

22. **confess** *Did anyone* **confess** *to the crime.* **confess**

23. **profess** *I don't* **profess** *to know everything.* **profess**

24. **press** *I might have to* **press** *the wrinkles out of my clothes.* **press**

25. **depress** *Wrinkles tend to* **depress** *me.* **depress**

Second Day

Have your children take out their *AVKO Student Response Book for Sequential Spelling* and turn to page 5. Or, if you're using your own paper, have your children take out their spelling folders with the papers you had them carefully fold the day before. Have them go to the second sheet where you had them write Lesson 2. The purpose is to keep them from using the words that they had the day before as a mental crutch.

Obviously, if your children have *the AVKO Student Response Book for Sequential Spelling* this problem does not exist because the second day slot is on page 3, the third day is on page 5, the fourth day on page 7, the fifth day on page 9, etc. You can begin by telling your children, "Today, the first word is:

gasses Oxygen and hydrogen are both gasses. gasses.

Does anybody know what the last two letters are in **gasses**? Did everybody double the letter **S**? **g-a** double the **s** and add –**es**.

Number two is **gasoline** as in: Yes, we had the word **gasoline** yesterday. **gasoline**.

Did we spell **gas** and then add an **o** and then **l-i-n-e** to get **gasoline**? If not, make it right.

Number 4 is **lasses**. The word lads goes with **lasses** just like the word boys goes with girls. **lasses**

Number 5 is **glasses**. Has anybody seen my **glasses**? **glasses**.

6. **classes** How many **classes** do you have? **classes**

7. **grasses** How many different kinds of **grasses** have you heard of? **grasses**

8. **passes** I have three extra **passes** for the next game. **passes**

9. **trespasses** A good hunter never **trespasses** on private property. **trespasses**

10. **surpasses** The offer of free coffee **surpasses** any previous offer. **surpasses**

11. **masses** St. Michael's church has three **masses** every Sunday. **masses**

12. **overpass** They're building a new **overpass**. **overpass**

13. **underpass** They should have built a better **underpass**. **underpass**

14. ***Les** My friend **Les** lost five pounds last month. **Les**

15. **messes** Nobody **messes** around with Leroy Brown. **messes**

16. **guesses** I'll give you three **guesses**. **guesses**

17. **dresses** She bought herself three new **dresses** for her birthday. **dresses**

18. **undressed** We generally get **undressed** before we go to bed. **undressed**

19. **processed** The caseworker **processed** the papers in record time. **processed**

20. **successes** We measure our **successes**, one student at a time.

21. * **blessed** We should be **blessed** with children not cursed by them.

22. **confessed** Who **confessed** to committing all those crimes? **confessed**

23. **professed** My professor **professed** his profession to be the best. **professed**

24. **presses** Stop the **presses**! **presses**

25. **depressed** It's no fun being **depressed**. **depressed**

* **Note:** These words are homophones. Les/less and blessed/blest. Use your own judgment as to whether or not to teach them now. If you're British, use your own judg**e**ment.

The Third Day

We begin the third day by having your children take out their *AVKO Student Response Book for Sequential Spelling* or by having them take their spelling sheet from their special folder. We feel that it is easier to have children open a response book to page 7 than it is to keep track of loose sheets of paper, but it can be done with the sheets successfully.

On this, the third day, you will begin the slow process of programming your children's God given computer brains to form the ending -*assed* correctly. There is no need at this time to encumber a child's mind with rules about added -*es* to words ending in -*s*, -*ch*, and -*sh*; or about doubling consonants. All we want to do is to have your children form the habit of spelling /ES iz/ -*esses*. But, for now, please do not go into any lectures about short vowels and long vowels. It's not at all necessary. In fact, it generally tends to confuse children. However, if one of your children asks about the rules, tell him that you will discuss the rules with him later – and keep your word. You can start by saying: **successes**

1. **gassed** Before we left, we **gassed** up the car. **gassed**   **blessed**

2. **gassy** If there's anything I hate, it's a **gassy** dog. **gassy**

3. **sassafras** Every once in a while I really enjoy **sassafras** tea. **sassafras**

4. **lassie** For every **lassie** there ought to be a laddie. **lassie**

5. **classy** Katherine Hepburn was known to be a **classy** person. **classy**

6. **classed** She has been **classed** as a great actress. **classed**

7. **passer** A winning football team needs a good **passer**. **passer**

8. * **passed** It's no fun to be **passed** up. * **passed**

9. **trespassed** We forgave those who **trespassed** against us. **trespassed**

10. **surpassed** We were **surpassed** by few. **surpassed**

11. * **massed** The people **massed** together in great big groups. ***massed**

12. **bluegrass** In Kentucky, the **bluegrass** is really green. **bluegrass**

13. **bypass** We took the **bypass** to avoid all the traffic. **bypass**

8

14. **Wes** My friend **Wes** does not like to be called Wesley. **Wes**

15. **messed** You shouldn't have **messed** with Leroy Brown. **messed**

16. * **guessed** You should have **guessed** that Leroy was big and bad.* **guessed**

17. **dressed** We got all **dressed** up for the party.**dressed**

18. * **less** We had a lot of fun, more or **less**. * **less**

19. **processing** I hate to spend time **processing** papers. **processing**

20. **successful** We were **successful** in getting through to the director. **successful**

21. **successive** We called him on five **successive** days. **successive**

22. **confessing** I guess we're **confessing** to being very persistent. **confessing**

23. **professor** I am sometimes called an absent-minded **professor**. **professor**

24. **pressed** Let's hurry up. I'm **pressed** for time. **pressed**

25. **depressing** Finishing a lesson shouldn't be **depressing**. **depressing**

* These words are homophones: passed/past; massed/mast; guessed/guest; Les/less.

The Fourth Day

The fourth day we begin by having the children take out their *AVKO Student Response Book for Sequential Spelling* and open it to page 9 or by having them take out their special spelling sheets. You can start by saying:

1.**gassing** Did you know **gassing** up your car is illegal in Oregon? **gassing**

2. **gasoline** Yes, I know self-service **gasoline** stations are illegal there. **gasoline**

3. **sassafras** There are only four *s*'s in "**sassafras** tea." **sassafras**

4. **lassies** Laddies go with **lassies**. **lassies**

5. **classiest** Kate Smith is my idea of the **classiest** singer. **classiest**

6. **classing** **Classing** means the same as classifying. **classing**

7. **passers** Quarterbacks need to be very good **passers**. **passers**

8. **passing** I hope you're not worried about getting a **passing** grade. **passing**

9. **trespassers** Yes, **trespassers** on private property can be prosecuted. **trespassers**

10. **surpassing** Your progress has been **surpassing** my fondest hopes. **surpassing**

11. **massing** The troops were **massing** together around the border. **massing**

12. **spyglass** **Spyglass** is an old-fashioned word for telescope. **spyglass**

13. **eyeglasses** In my family, we all wear **eyeglasses**.

14. **dresser** Beau Brummel was a very snappy **dresser**. **dresser**

15. **messing** You had better stop **messing** around, Mr. Messer. **messing**

16.* **guessing** I hope you're not * **guessing** how to spell this word. * **guessing**

17. **dressing** The tomato blushed when she saw the salad **dressing**. **dressing**

18. **unless** **Unless** you get up, you're not going anywhere. **unless**

19. **processed** All the parts of the chicken went into the **processed** meat. **processed**

20. **successfully** Jan, Jane, and Janet all **successfully** completed the test. **successfully**

21. **succession** They filed in one-by-one in perfect **succession. succession**

22. **confession** The dying man made a death bed **confession. confession**

23. **profession** Teaching should be considered an honorable **profession. profession**

24. **pressing** We shall be **pressing** forward. **pressing**

---

25. **depression** When I was growing up, the U.S. was in a depression
depression
essi ("ESH") ession ("ESH un")
de + pr + ession = depression
Before showing this, check your children's papers to see if they have learned to spell the word *depression*. Almost every child should have spelled **depression** correctly. Now, compare this spelling to the misspellings you collected on the first day. Tell your students you are proud of them. Tell them that they have learned a difficult word without ever having studied the word. Tell them that just by paying attention in class and correcting their mistakes they are learning and learning a great deal.

---

* gu: In words such as guess, guest, guilty, guile, guide, Guernsey, guild, etc. the letters gu are really a consonant digraph! The letter u is silent but it still functions as a signal that the gu is a hard /g/. Many teachers forget this and treat the ue and ui in these words as a vowel digraph. Please don't. The letter u after the g in these words goes with the g to make it hard.

The Fifth Day

On the 5th day we begin by having the children take out their *AVKO Student Response Book for Sequential Spelling* or by having them take out their special spelling folder and finding the sheet with Lesson 5 on it. Then give the following words in sentences:

1. **impress** What do I have to do to **impress** you? **impress**

2. **compress** To **compress** something is to make it smaller. **compress**

3. **decompress** To **decompress** is to bring back to its original size. **decompress**

4. **oppress** It's wrong to **oppress** any group of people. **oppress**

5. **express** Did I just **express** my personal opinion? **express** depression

6. **stress** We should **stress** doing right and avoid doing wrong. **stress**

7. **distress** Flying a flag upside down is a standard **distress** signal. **distress**

8. **assess** Sometimes it's difficult to **assess** the damage done. **assess**

9. **nevertheless** **Nevertheless** sounds like three words, but it's only one. **nevertheless**

10. **bench-press** Johnny Joe can **bench-press** 200 pounds. **bench-press**

11. **possess** I think you **possess** the skill to spell this word. **possess**

12. ** **progress** I really think you're making very good **progress. progress**

13. ** **progress** When you go forward, you **progress** (pruh GRESS). **progress**

14. **kiss** Little children should always receive a **kiss** good-night. **kiss**

15. **miss** I hate to **miss** my favorite TV program. **miss**

16. **dismiss** I am not about to **dismiss** this class right now. **dismiss**

17. * **amiss** There's something **amiss** about that girl. **amiss**

18. **a Miss** Smith Is there **a Miss** Smith in this room? **a Miss** Smith

19. **bus** Can you find **us** in a **bus**? **bus**

20. **pus** When you can see **pus**, you know your wound is infected. **pus**

21. **plus** When can 11 **plus** 2 equal 1? (When we talking clock time!!! Eleven o'clock plus 2 hours makes it one o'clock.) **plus**

22. **fuss** What is all that **fuss** about? **fuss**

23. **cuss** I really hate to hear anyone **cuss**. **cuss**

24. **discuss** If you want to know why, we can **discuss** that later. **discuss**

25. **truss** We need one more roof **truss** put up so we can start. **truss**

The Sixth Day

The 6th day we begin by having the children take out their *AVKO Student Response Book for Sequential Spelling* and open it to page 13 or by having them take out their special spelling sheet. Then give the following words in sentences:

1. **impressed** Your progress in spelling has really **impressed** me. **impressed**

2. **compresses** An air compressor **compresses** air. **compresses**

3. **decompressed** The air in his lungs had to be **decompressed**. **decompressed**

4. **oppressed** The Catholics in Northern Ireland believe they have been **oppressed** for centuries. **oppressed**

5. **expressed** The Protestants have **expressed** a different opinion. **expressed**

6. **stressed** Our minister has always **stressed** reading the Bible daily. **stressed**

7. **distressed** He was quite **distressed** when he found his son cheating. **distressed**

8. **assessed** The assessor **assessed** the value of our house too high. **assessed**

9. **Bess Bess** wore a brand new dress to church. **Bess**

10. **access** We told the contractor we wanted easy **access** to the attic. **access**

11. **possessed** Whatever **possessed** you to tell such a whopper? **possessed**

12. **hard-pressed** She was **hard-pressed** to find an answer. **hard-pressed**

13. **progressed** We have **progressed** from simple to difficult words. **progressed**

14. **kisses** Hershey makes candy **kisses**. **kisses**

15. * **misses** Miss Smith really **misses** her boyfriend. **misses**

16. * **Mrs.** Smith **Mrs.** Smith doesn't ever miss going to church on Sunday. **Mrs. Smith**

17. **dismisses** If she ever **dismisses** the class, let's go get a sundae. **dismisses**

18. **hiss** It's not polite to **hiss**. That's what snakes do. **hiss**

19. * **buses** School **buses** are really quite safe to ride on. **buses**

20. * **busses** If she **busses busses**, she kisses buses. **busses**

21. **thus** It has always been **thus**. **thus**

22. **fusses** When a baby **fusses**, it may need to be fed, changed, burped, or cuddled. **fusses**

23. **cusses** When someone **cusses** me out, I don't pay any attention. **cusses**

24. **discusses** When someone **discusses** something with me, I listen. **discusses**

25. **trusses** The roof required twenty **trusses**. **trusses**

Homophones: Mrs./misses/missus/miss us   bus/buss   buses/busses

Note: The preferred plural of *bus* is *buses*, but it is acceptable to spell it "busses."

Note: The preferred past tense of *bus* is *bused*, but it is acceptable to spell it "bussed."

The Seventh Day

We begin the 7th day by having them open their *AVKO Student Response Books* for *Sequential Spelling* to page 15 or by having them take out their special spelling sheets.

1. **impressive** Your progress in spelling is very, very **impressive**. **impressive**

2. **compressing** *Moby Dick* needs a great deal of **compressing**. **compressing**

3. **decompresses** A decompression chamber **decompresses** the air in the lungs. **decompresses**

4. **oppressive** Dictatorships produce **oppressive** governments. **oppressive**

5. **expressive** Good actors have very **expressive** faces. **expressive**

6. **stresses** Prayer can help a person overcome the **stresses** of life. **stresses**

7. **excessive** Anything that is **excessive** can lead to evil. **excessive**

8. **assessment** At least that was the rabbi's **assessment**. **assessment**

9. **chess** I wonder if the apostles ever played **chess**. **chess**

10. **Tess Tess** thinks she is a better chess player than I am.   **Tess**

11. **possessive** Little children are naturally quite **possessive**. Mine! **possessive**

12. **duress** A contract signed under **duress** is not legally binding. **duress**

13. **progressive** Being **progressive** may not always be best. **progressive**

14. **kissed** I think that politician has **kissed** a thousand babies. **kissed**

15.* **missed** We were late because we **missed** the bus. **missed**

16. **dismissed** The judge **dismissed** the lawsuit as frivolous. **dismissed**

17. **Swiss** The **Swiss** miss came from Switzerland. **Swiss**

18. **hissed** The audience **hissed** when the villain came on stage. **hissed**

19. * **bused** Some children are **bused** across town to go to school. **bused**

20. * **bussed** Other children are **bussed** to nearby towns. **bussed**

21. **supposed to** You're **supposed to** get me to the church on time. **supposed to** Please use normal sloppy speech and pronounce supposed to as "SPOH stuh" "You're sposta git me to the church on time." **"Sposta"**

22 **fussed** You shouldn't have **fussed** so much over nothing. **fussed**

23. **cussed** The sergeant **cussed** out the new recruit. **cussed**

24. * **discussed** The chaplain **discussed** that with the sergeant. **discussed**

25. **buss** An old-fashioned word for kiss is **buss**. **buss**

* **Homophones**: bused / bussed / bust discussed / disgust ("almost" homophonic)

After the Seventh Day

After the seventh day, I include a 25 word spelling test. Some days the tests are easier than others, but don't panic on days like the

12

124th day when the word *apprehension* is presented.

REMEMBER: My learning philosophy is *not* concerned about teaching the spelling of any one word *per se*. I am concerned with the teaching of basic sounds for both spelling and reading. In the case of words like *suspend, suspension; comprehend, comprehension; apprehend, apprehension; pretend, pretension; extend, extension; pension*, I feel that teaching the *–end/ension* endings, prefixes, as well as the initial consonant sounds and consonant blends, is important.

REMEMBER: Encourage your students to **speed** through these tests. Give the word. Put it in a sentence. Say the word. Spell the word. Have the students (if you can) trace the corrected spelling as they spell it aloud in group chorus. Go on to the next —but make sure your students make an attempt at the spelling *before* you give the correct spelling. **Copying** your spelling does **not** help them learn. **Correcting** their own misspelling **does**.

Immediate Feedback

The most common mistake made in administering the *AVKO Sequential Spelling Tests* is to give the entire test and then correct. This method just **won't** work.

- Give each word separately.
- Say the word. Give it in a sentence.
- Let the students attempt the spelling.
- Give the correct spelling. Let students correct their mistakes.
- Then give the next word. Repeat the process of immediate student self-correction.

Grading

If you desire to give grades for spelling, I would recommend that you give tests for grading purposes separately. You may then grade your students on their learning of the spelling of the sounds—not the words. Sequential Spelling gives permission for parents (and teachers) to duplicate (for their students only) the tests that come after the 40th, 80th, 120th, 160th and 180th days. Read the sentences to your students. All they have to do is fill in the blanks. Notice that you are not testing on the whole word. You are testing only on the spelling patterns taught. (That is why the initial consonants or blends are given to the student.) NOTE: You can use these as a pre-tests, as well as post-tests, to show progress. How you grade these tests is up to you. I recommend that 0-2 wrong = A, 3-4 = B, 5-6 = C, and 7-8 = D.

If your students get more than 8 wrong, I recommend going back over the process to help them learn what they are missing.

Questions most frequently asked concerning Sequential Spelling

1. What are those asterisks (*) and exclamation marks doing next to some words?

The asterisks merely serve as a reminder to the parent/teacher that the word so marked has a **homophone** (same pronunciation, different spelling), has a **heteronym** (same spelling, different word and different pronunciation), or does not follow the normal pattern. For example, *gyp* ** should logically be spelled *"jip."* But instead of *j* we use the letter *"g."* Instead of *i* the letter *y* is used. Likewise, the word *proper* ** should logically be spelled *"propper"* just like *hopper*, and *copper*, and *stopper*, but it isn't.

2. Why don't the words used follow grade levels? For example, *nephew* is an *8th* grade word in many school's regular spelling texts.

Regular spelling texts, as a general rule, pick grade levels for words according to when the words first begin to occur in the curriculum. This would seem to make sense, but it does bring about some rather odd sequences. Since the word *ice* may not occur in the curriculum until the fourth grade (when it appears in the science class), its introduction is delayed until that time even though *nice* may occur in the first grade, *twice* in the second grade, *price* in the fifth, and *rice* in the sixth.

We believe in teaching the phonics necessary for decoding through the back door of spelling and without preaching rules that may or may not be useful. We teach the word *nephew* only after the *–ew "yoo"* sound has been taught in 12 different words. Notice that the word nephew directly after the homophones **few** and **phew**!

3. Why do you have so many words that are outside the vocabulary of normal adults, such as the word "mote"?

We don't believe it hurts anyone to learn a new word—but that is not why we use it. We use the word *mote* as an added practice in sounding out spellings of words having the initial /m/ sound and practice in spelling the ending *-ote*. It also gives the student a pleasant surprise and ego boost when he discovers he can spell a word that he believes he has never heard nor seen before—just because he knows how to spell the sounds.

4. Should I count off for sloppy handwriting?

Since the students get to correct their own spelling, they should be expected to write clearly and legibly. In fact, I recommend that these sequential spelling tests be used for handwriting practice because the patterns, being repetitive, can be a help in developing legible handwriting. I further recommend that if your students print, that they use D'Nealian® manuscript. If your students write, we strongly recommend D'Nealian® cursive. Another excellent system is the Italic by Getty-Dubay. But whatever system you use, we believe that **writing must be legible**. So, yes, by all means, take off for sloppy handwriting (provided the student has no physical disability and has sufficient small motor skills to write legibly).

5. Do I have to use all the words that are in the tests? Can I drop some? Can I change some?

No, you don't have to use them all. You can drop some. You know your children better than I do. Yes, you can substitute other words for the ones I have selected. *The Patterns of English Spelling* is your best reference to select from. If, for example, you would rather start with the -at, bat, rat, cat, sat family, be my guest. You can use your pencil to write in your choices. Every student is different. Don't be afraid to trust your own judgment.

6. Can I give the same test more than once during the day?

Yes. If your students can profit from that, fine. I recommend, however, that you allow a minimum of two hours to pass between re-tests.

I also recommend four as the absolute maximum number of times that Sequential Spelling be given in one day, whether repeats or new lessons.

7. I have a child who is a 5th grader. May I use Sequential Spelling 1 to start one hour, Sequential Spelling 2 to start the 2nd hour, 3 for the third, etc.? I want my child to become as good a reader and speller as possible.

Why not? If it works, it works. If it doesn't, then try something else. You could try going through four days of Sequential Spelling I every day until it is finished and then move through four days of Sequential Spelling II every day, and continue on through four levels of Sequential Spelling in one year.

8. Why are some words in bold print?

The words in **bold print** are those that are the most commonly used words and the most important to learn. You will also notice that some words (like the word **doesn't**) that don't follow regular patterns are repeated many times throughout the series. If your students learn to spell any of the words that are not in bold face, that is a bonus. What I want the students to learn is to spell the most common words and to learn the most common patterns that occur in words. You will discover that most of these patterns consist of only two, three, or four letters. A big word like *misunderstandings* can be broken into the following patterns: *mis/un/der/st/and/ing/s*.

9. Do I have to teach all the homophones and homographs listed?

Absolutely not. I have listed them for your convenience. If you wish to teach them, fine. If you don't, fine. I only ask that when they come up that you definitely use the word in a sentence that helps the student pick the right word. For example: Don't just say **billed**. The students may think about the word **build**. Instead, say something like: "**billed**. *We were* **billed** *for extra carpeting.* **billed**.*"

10. What does TPES stand for at the bottom of the pages?

TPES stands for *The Patterns of English Spelling*. This book contains all the words that share a common spelling pattern placed on the same page (or pages in the case of families like the -tion family). In our Sequential Spelling Series, I list most of the words in each family, but not all. If a parent/teacher wants to include more or wants to give special assignments to the gifted students, I have included the page references. This book may be purchased from the AVKO Educational Research Foundation, 3084 W. Willard Rd., Clio, MI 48420. For more information call toll free: 1-866-AVKO 612.

11. Can I use the words in Sequential Spelling for composition?

Yes, of course. Having your students create sentences out of the words is good exercise for their minds and will allow you to determine if they truly understand what the words really mean. You may also have them write the entire sentence that you dictate. That will help you help them handle the problems created by speech patterns, such as the "wanna" instead of "want to" and the "whacha gonna" for "what are you going to," etc. As the parent/teacher, you know your students and how many sentences they can handle as homework. You might even want to set time limits such as: Write as many sentences using today's spelling words as you can in 10 minutes.

12. Is there anything I can use to help my students' reading that will also reinforce the spelling?

AVKO's *New Word Families in Sentence Context* may be used in conjunction with Sequential Spelling. The page number given for *The Patterns of English Spelling* (TPES) also works for the *Word Families in Sentence Context*. This book may also be obtained from the AVKO Educational Research Foundation. If you have any questions feel free to call 866-AVKO-612 or E-mail info@avko.org

	1st day	2nd day	3rd day	4th day
1.	**gas**	gasses	gassed	gassing
2.	gasoline	gasoline	gassy	gasoline
3.	* alas	alas	sassafras	sassafras
4.	* a lass	lasses	lassie	lassies
5.	**glass**	**glasses**	classy	classiest
6.	class	classes	classed	classing
7.	**grass**	grasses	passer	passers
8.	pass	passes	* **passed**	passing
9.	trespass	trespasses	trespassed	trespassers
10.	surpass	surpasses	surpassed	surpassing
11.	mass	masses	* massed	massing
12.	** bass	overpass	bluegrass	spyglass
13.	**brass**	underpass	bypass	eyeglasses
14.	**yes**	* Les	* Wes	dresser
15.	mess	messes	messed	messing
16.	**guess**	**guesses**	* **guessed**	guessing
17.	**dress**	dresses	dressed	**dressing**
18.	undress	undressed	* less	**unless**
19.	process	processed	processing	processed
20.	**success**	successes	**successful**	successfully
21.	bless	* **blessed**	successive	succession
22.	confess	confessed	confessing	confession
23.	profess	professed	professor	profession
24.	press	presses	pressed	pressing
25.	depress	depressed	depressing	depression

* Homophones:

alas/a lass	Alas, it was a lass and not a lad that won the tournament.
passed/past	When we passed through Chicago, it was way past midnight.
massed/mast	The men in *Moby Dick* were massed around the mast of the ship.
Wes/west	Wes is short for Wesley. Cleveland is west of Albany.
Les/less	Les is short for Lester, more or less.
blessed/blest	We were blessed (or blest) as the case may be.
guessed/guest	The guest guessed correctly to wait for the host to begin eating.

* Heteronyms: bass ("bass")/bass ("BAY'ss") We went fishing for bass. Jack sang bass.

See the complete -ass family on p. 156 in *The Patterns of English Spelling* (TPES); the -aw, p. 319.

	5th day	6th day	7th day	8th day
1.	impress	**impressed**	impressive	impression
2.	compress	compresses	compressing	compression
3.	decompress	decompressed	decompresses	decompression
4.	oppress	oppressed	oppressive	oppression
5.	express	expressed	expressive	expression
6.	**stress**	stressed	stresses	stressing
7.	distress	excess	excessive	lesson
8.	assess	assessed	assessment	assessor
9.	nevertheless	Bess	chess	housedress
10.	bench-press	access	Tess	Bess
11.	**possess**	possessed	possessive	possession
12.**	made **progress**	hard-pressed	duress	Miss Hess
13.	** to progress	progressed	progressive	progression
14.	**kiss**	**kisses**	**kissed**	kissing
15.	**miss**	misses	* missed	missing
16.	dismiss	dismisses	dismissed	dismissal
17.	* amiss	hit-and-miss	Swiss	bliss
18.	a Miss Smith	hiss	hissed	hissing
19.	**bus**	buses	* bused	busing
20.	pus	busses	* bussed	bussing
21.	**plus**	thus	beauty	beautiful
22.	**fuss**	fusses	fussed	fussing
23.	cuss	cusses	cussed	cussing
24.	**discuss**	**discusses**	**discussed**	discussion
25.	truss	trusses	*** buss	focus

* Homophones:

missed/mist	When the mayor of London visited Arizona, he said he missed the mist.
bussed/bust/bused.	The bust of Shakespeare was bused (or bussed) from school to school.
amiss/a miss	What do you call something wrong with a girl? Something amiss with a miss.

** Heteronyms:
progress n. ("PRAH gress")/progress v. ("proh GRESS")

*** NOTES: The word buss means to kiss.

See the complete -iss family on p. 158 in *The Patterns of English Spelling* (TPES);
the -uss, p. 160; the -us, p. 160.

	9th day	10th day	11th day	12th day
1.	**best**	pest	west	* blest
2.	**nest**	nests	nested	nesting
3.	**test**	tests	tested	testing
4.	detest	detests	detested	detesting
5.	protest	protests	protested	protesting
6.	attest	attests	attested	attesting
7.	**rest**	rests	rested	resting
8.	arrest	arrests	arrested	arresting
9.	vest	vests	zest	zestful
10.	invest	invests	invested	investment
11.	**suggest**	suggests	suggested	**suggestion**
12.	digest	digests	digested	digestion
13.	congest	congested	congestive	congestion
14.	infest	infested	one * **guest**	two guests
15.	Eve	Eve's apple	**even**	**evening**
16.	Steve	Steve's apple	* Steven	* Stevenson
17.	peeve	Joyce Steeves	(**) * Stephen	* Stephenson
18.	**sleeve**	sleeves	pet peeves	beauty
19.	**seven**	sevens	seventy	seventy-seven
20.	**eleven**	elevens	heaven	heavens
21.	leaven	leavens	leavened	unleavened
22.	**ever**	whatever	whatsoever	wherever
23.	lever	clever	whenever	whoever
24.	whoever	however	**forever**	**beautiful**
25.	sever	severed	severing	**several**

* Homophones:

blest/blessed	They were blest (or blessed) as the case may be.
guest/guessed	You guessed right. The speaker was my guest.
Steven/Stephen	Is it Steven or Stephen whose last name is Stephenson?
Stevenson/Stephenson	Steven's son is Steve Stevenson; Stephen's son is Steve Stephenson.

*** NOTE: The test in attest is similar to that in testimony, testify, and testament.

See the complete -est family on p. 234 in *The Patterns of English Spelling* (TPES); the -eve, p. 324; the -even, p. 339; -ever, 669.

	13th day	14th day	15th day	16th day
1.	thief	thieves	thief	thieving
2.	**belief**	believes	beliefs	believing
3.	**brief**	briefs	briefed	briefly
4.	debrief	debriefs	debriefed	debriefing
5.	**chief**	chiefs	chiefly	beauties
6.	kerchief	kerchiefs	neckerchief	neckerchiefs
7.	handkerchief	handkerchiefs	**mischief**	**mischievous**
8.	**relief**	relieves	relieving	relief
9.	**grief**	grieves	grieving	briefcase
10.	achieve	achieves	achieving	achievement
11.	**leave**	leaf	leaves	**leaving**
12.	weave	weaves	weaving	deceit
13.	* eave	eaves	! receipt	receipts
14.	heave	heaves	heaved	heaving
15.	**receive**	**receives**	**receiving**	**reception**
16.	deceive	deceives	deceiving	deception
17.	perceive	perceives	perceived	perception
18.	conceive	conceived	inconceivable	conception
19.	preconceive	preconceived	misconceived	preconception
20.	jazz	jazzes	jazzed	jazzing
21.	razz	razzes	razzed	razzing
22.	razzmatazz	isn't	wasn't	hasn't
23.	**quiz**	quizzes	quizzed	quizzing
24.	whiz	whizzes	whizzed	whizzing
25.	fizz	fizzes	fizzed	fizzing

* Homophones:

Eve/eave   Did Eve stand under the eave?

Note: The letters *f* and *v* play switchie-switchie as in belief/believe; life/lives; wolf/wolves; shelf/shelves; etc.

See the complete -ief family on p. 406 in *The Patterns of English Spelling* (TPES); the -ieve, p. 441; the -ceive, p. 441; -azz, p. 136; -izz, p. 138.

19

	17th day	18th day	19th day	20th day
1.	fuzz	fuzzy	fuzzier	fuzziest
2.	buzz	buzzes	buzzed	buzzing
3.	buzzer	buzzers	buzzard	buzzards
4.	**puzzle**	puzzles	puzzled	puzzling
5.	muzzle	muzzles	muzzled	muzzling
6.	**does**	doesn't	was	wasn't
7.	**rifle**	rifles	rifled	rifling
8.	trifle	trifles	trifled	trifling
9.	stifle	stifles	stifled	stifling
10.	**stiff**	stiffs	stiffer	stiffest
11.	sniff	sniffs	sniffed	sniffing
12.	cliff	cliffs	skiff	skiffs
13.	whiff	whiffs	whiffed	whiffing
14.	**sheriff**	sheriffs	the sheriff's badge	sheriff
15.	tariff	tariffs	mastiff	mastiffs
16.	tiff	tiffs	riff	miff
17.	plaintiff	plaintiffs	mischief	handkerchief
18.	**puff**	puffs	puffed	puffing
19.	**stuff**	stuffs	**stuffed**	**stuffing**
20.	* **ruff**	ruffs	ruffed	ruffing
21.	cuff	**cuffs**	cuffed	cuffing
22.	handcuff	handcuffs	handcuffed	handcuffing
23.	scuff	scuffs	**scuffed**	scuffing
24.	**bluff**	bluffs	**bluffed**	**bluffing**
25.	**suffer**	**suffers**	**suffered**	**suffering**

* Homophones:
ruff/rough   It can be rough if your opponents ruff your ace.

See the complete -uzz family on p. 140 in *The Patterns of English Spelling* (TPES);
the -ifle, p. 612; -iff, p. 143; -uff, p. 145.

	21st day	22nd day	23rd day	24th day
1.	*** air**	airs	aired	airing
2.	*** pair**	pairs	paired	pairing
3.	**chair**	chairs	chaired	chairing
4.	*** hair**	hairs	red-haired	fair-haired
5.	*** fair**	fairs	**unfair**	unfairly
6.	repair	repairs	**repaired**	repairing
7.	impair	impairs	impaired	impairment
8.	despair	despairs	despaired	despairing
9.	airport	airline	airsick	hairball
10.	**stairs**	stairway	stair steps	upstairs
11.	*** wear**	wears	wore/worn	wearing
12.	**swear**	swears	swore/sworn	swearing
13.	*** (**) tear**	tears	tore/torn	tearing
14.	*** pear**	pears	sportswear	underwear
15.	*** bear**	bears	bore/borne	bearing
16.	*** heir**	heirs	heirloom	heiress
17.	* their * heir	It was * theirs.	* Your * heir	* It's * theirs.
18.	**care**	cares	cared	caring
19.	**scare**	scares	**scared**	scaring
20.	**dare**	dares	dared	daring
21.	* bare	* bares	* bared	* baring
22.	**stare**	*** stares**	stared	staring
23.	**share**	shares	shared	sharing
24.	**spare**	spares	spared	sparing
25.	**square**	squares	squared	squaring

* Homophones:

fair/fare	What do you call a just ticket price? A fair fare.
they're/their/there	They're going to build their house over there.
there's/theirs	There's something special about everything that is theirs.
you're/your/yore	You're going to discover your ancestors lived in the days of yore.
it's/its	It's too bad the dog couldn't catch its tail.
Eire/air/heir	What do you call an Irishman who inherits a windbag? An Eire air heir.
pear/pair	What do you call a couple of Bartletts? A pear pair.
hare/hair	What do you call rabbit fur? Hare hair.
ware/wear	What do you call clothing for sale? Wear ware.
bare/bear	What do you call a naked grizzlie? A bare bear.
tare/tear	What do you call the weight of a rip? The tare tear.

* Heteronyms:

tear "TEER"/tear "TAY'r"   We shed a tear or two when we saw how big a tear there was in the tent.

See the complete -eck family on p. 215 in *The Patterns of English Spelling*; the -awk, p. 215.

	25th day	26th day	27th day	28th day
1.	* fare	fares	fared	faring
2.	welfare	airfare	warfare	bus fare
3.	* pare	pares	pared	paring
4.	prepare	prepares	prepared	preparing
5.	compare	compares	compared	comparing
6.	glare	glares	glared	glaring
7.	snare	snares	snared	snaring
8.	* ware	wares	hardware	software
9.	silverware	cookware	aware	unaware
10.	* flare	flares	flared	flaring
11.	* mare	* mares	rare	rarely
12.	* beware	Delaware	bareback	barefoot
13.	scarce	scarcely	scarce	scarcely
14.	word	words	worded	wording
15.	reword	reworded	password	* foreword
16.	work	works	worked	working
17.	workers	workable	workbench	workbook
18.	* world	worlds	worldly	world-wide
19.	worm	worms	wormed	worming
20.	silkworm	wormy	wormhole	tapeworm
21.	worry	worries	worried	worrying
22.	worrywart	worrisome	worse	worst
23.	worship	worships	worshipped	worshipping
24.	worth	worthless	worthwhile	worthiness
25.	patchwork	fireworks	woodworking	worshipper

* Homophones:

fair/fare	Honest prices for travel would be fair fare.
pair/pear/pare	Two is a pair. A pear is a fruit. You can pare an apple or a potato.
beware/bee wear	What is a warning about honey gatherers clothing? Beware bee wear.
wear/ware	What do you call clothing? Wear ware.
flare/flair	What do you call a penchant for lighting up the skies? A flare flair.
mare/mayor	What do you call a horse that heads up a city? A mare mayor.
forward/foreword	What do you call a fresh preface? A forward foreword.
world/whirled	What do you call a spinning earth? A whirled world.

See the complete -ax family on p. 265 in *The Patterns of English Spelling* (TPES); the -ix, p. 267; the -ox, p. 268; the -oax, p. 268; -ast, p. 233.

	29th day	30th day	31st day	32nd day
1.	**large**	largely	larger	largest
2.	**charge**	charges	charged	charging
3.	recharge	recharged	charger	enlarger
4.	enlarge	enlarged	enlargement	enlarging
5.	discharge	discharged	discharging	surcharge
6.	overcharge	undercharge	barge	barges
7.	Marge	margin	marginal	marginally
8.	**soup**	soups	soupy	soups
9.	**group**	groups	grouped	trouping
10.	regroup	regroups	regrouped	regrouping
11.	recoup	recoups	recouped	recouping
12.	soup-to-nuts	soup meat	soupspoon	coupon
13.	**rip**	rips	**ripped**	ripping
14.	**trip**	trips	**tripped**	tripping
15.	**strip**	strips	stripped	stripping
16.	grip	grips	gripped	gripping
17.	**drip**	drips	dripped	dripping
18.	**tip**	tips	tipped	tipping
19.	**lip**	lips	lipped	lipping
20.	**slip**	slips	slipped	**slippers**
21.	clip	clips	clipped	clippers
22.	flip	flips	flipped	flipping
23.	**dip**	dips	dipped	dipper
24.	sip	snips	sipped	snipping
25.	**whip**	whips	**whipped**	**whipping**

See the complete -arge family on p. 507 in *The Patterns of English Spelling* (TPES); the -ip, p. 128.

	33rd day	34th day	35th day	36th day
1.	skip	skips	skipped	skipper
2.	**chip**	**chips**	chipped	chipping
3.	**ship**	ships	shipped	shipping
4.	gyp	gyps	gypped	gypping
5.	gypsy	gypsies	turnips	tightlipped
6.	tulip	* **tulips**	horsewhip	horsewhipped
7.	worship	worships	* worshipped	* worshipping
8.	zip	unzipped	zipper	zippers
9.	gossip	gossips	*** gossiping	*** gossiping
10.	battleship	parsnips	*** * worshiped	*** * worshiping
11.	partnership	spaceship	hardship	friendship
12.	relationship	fingertips	*** * worshipers	* worshippers
13.	**top**	topped	topping	*** proper
14.	**stopped**	stopping	stopper	*** properly
15.	popped	popping	popper	*** property
16.	slop	slops	slopped	sloppy
17.	cops	**copper**	chopping	chopper
18.	**hop**	hops	**hopped**	**hopping**
19.	mop	mops	mopped	mopping
20.	drop	drops	dropped	dropping
21.	crop	crops	*** **proper**	*** **improper**
22.	prop	props	propped	propping
23.	*** **copy**	*** **copies**	*** **copied**	*** **copying**
24.	*** **photocopy**	*** **photocopies**	*** **copier**	*** **copiers**
25.	*** **miscopy**	*** **miscopies**	*** **miscopied**	*** **miscopying**

* Homophones:

tulips/two lips	What flowers can you always find right under your nose? Tulips.
worshipped/worshiped	Most of us worshipped; some of us worshiped.
worshipping/worshiping	Most of us were worshipping; some of us were worshiping.
worshippers/worshipers	Most of us were worshippers; some of us were worshipers.

*** Apparent Exceptions: The words *gossip*, *proper*, *copy*, etc. differ from other -ip and -op words in two ways. First, each base cannot be reduced to one syllable. Secondly, because of this, the letter p does not double. In the word *worship*, we have a bit of disagreement; you can double or not double. Be consistent.

See the complete -ip family on p. 128 in *The Patterns of English Spelling* (TPES); the -op, p. 129.

	37th day	38th day	39th day	40th day
1.	whopper	floppy	poppy	poppies
2.	nonstop	raindrops	blacktop	floppies
3.	eavesdrop	lollipops	pork chops	window-shopping
4.	ash	ashes	cashier	cashiers
5.	**cash**	cashes	cashed	cashing
6.	**trash**	trashes	trashed	trashing
7.	thrash	thrashes	thrashed	thrashing
8.	lash	clashes	flashed	dashing
9.	splash	splashes	splashed	splashing
10.	mash	smashes	mashed	smashing
11.	stash	stashes	stashed	hashing
12.	*** **wash**	**washes**	**washed**	**washing**
13.	*** **fashion**	fashions	old-fashioned	old-fashioned
14.	washer	washers	Washington	wishy-washy
15.	**wish**	**wishes**	wished	wishing
16.	**dish**	**dishes**	dished	dishing
17.	**fish**	fished	fishing	fisherman
18.	swish	swished	swishing	goldfish
19.	shellfish	jellyfish	catfish	starfish
20.	**selfish**	selfishly	unselfish	unselfishly
21.	**rush**	rushes	**rushed**	rushing
22.	**brush**	**brushes**	brushed	brushing
23.	crush	crushes	**crushed**	crushing
24.	**blush**	blushed	**blushing**	crusher
25.	flush	gushes	hushed	flushing

*** Apparent Exceptions:

wash   W-Control over the letter A gives the "AH" sound. See p. 504 in *The Patterns of English Spelling* (TPES)

fashion   SHI = "SH;" ON = "UN." The "AA - SHUN" sound can be spelled three ways: -a + ti + on as in ration, -a + ssi + on as in passion. Compare the spelling of the "shun" sound in fashion (shion) to the the spelling of the "shun" sound in cushion (shion) in the next set of lessons.

See the complete -ash family on p. 209 in *The Patterns of English Spelling* (TPES);
the -ish, p. 210; the -ush, p. 211.

Grading

If your particular system requires that a grade be given for spelling, we would recommend that tests for grading purposes be given at a separate time and that the children be graded on their learning of the spelling of the sounds – not the words as the suggested tests for grading purposes are constructed to do. AVKO gives permission for parents (and teachers) to duplicate for classroom purposes only the tests on the following pages. Read the sentences to your children. All they have to do is fill in the blanks. Notice that you are not testing on the whole word. You are testing only on the spelling patterns taught. That is why the initial consonants or blends are given to the children. Note: You can use this as a pre-test as well as a post-test to show real gains. How you grade these tests is up to you. Or use the 0-1 wrong = A, 2-3 = B, 4-5 = C, 5-6 = D. We don't expect that you'll have any E's.

Evaluation Test #1 (After 40 Days)

#	Sentence	Pattern being tested	Lesson word is in
1.	Has that suspect conf**essed** to the murder yet?	essed	2
2.	I hope we don't have another depr**ession**.	ession	4
3.	I have not dism**issed** this class yet.	issed	7
4.	We'll have a group disc**ussion** tomorrow.	ussion	8
5.	What was that group prot**esting** over?	esting	12
6.	I would like to make a sugg**estion**.	estion	12
7.	The policeman caught the th**ief** red-handed.	ief	13
8.	We bel**ieve*** you.	ieve	14
9.	I love going to wedding re**ceptions***.	ceptions	16
10.	I am really p**uzzled** by your reaction.	uzzled	19
11.	There is too much s**uffering** in this world.	uffering	20
12.	We should have our roof rep**aired** before it leaks.	aired	23
13.	I wish you would stop st**aring** at me.	aring	24
14.	We were prep**ared** for almost any emergency.	ared	27
15.	I wish you would stop comp**aring** me to my sister.	aring	28
16.	Do you know the pass**wor**d?	wor	27
17.	We were really **worried** about you.	wor	27
18.	Yes, they called a ch**arging** foul on Michael Jordan.	arging	32
19.	I can remember the last time I got a wh**ipping**.	ipping	32
20.	My cousin sk**ipped** the fourth grade.	ipped	35

* These words were never given, but other forms of these words were used.

Name_____ Date_____

Evaluation Test #1

Please, please, please do NOT start until your teacher gives you the directions.
You must stay with your teacher as she reads the sentences.
All you have to do is to fill in the blanks with the missing letters.

1. Has that suspect con_____ to the murder yet?

2. I hope we don't have another depr_____.

3. I have not dism_____ this class yet.

4. We'll have a group disc_____ tomorrow.

5. What was that group prot_____ over?

6. I would like to make a sugg_____.

7. The policeman caught the th_____ red-handed.

8. We bel_____ you.

9. I love going to wedding re_____ .

10. I am really p_____by your reaction.

11. There is too much s_____ in this world.

12. We should have our roof rep_____ before it leaks.

13. I wish you would stop st_____ at me.

14. We were pre_____ for almost any emergency.

15. I wish you would stop com_____ me to my sister.

16. Do you know the pass_____d?

17. We were really _____ried about you.

18. Yes, they called a ch_____ foul on Michael Jordan.

19. I can remember the last time I got a wh_____ .

20. My cousin sk_____ the fourth grade.

	41st day	42nd day	43rd day	44th day
1.	**push**	pushes	pushed	pushing
2.	**bush**	**bushes**	bushed	bushing
3.	ambush	ambushes	ambushed	ambushing
4.	bushel	bushels	pincushion	pincushions
5.	cushion	cushions	cushioned	cushioning
6.	**door**	doors	beautiful	beautifully
7.	**floor**	floors	floored	flooring
8.	subfloor	subfloors	subflooring	beauties
9.	outdoor	outdoors	indoor	indoors
10.	next-door	trapdoor	out-of-doors	doorknob
11.	doormat	door prize	doorway	doorstop
12.	doorstep	doorman	doorbell	poorhouse
13.	* **poor**	poorly	poorer	poorest
14.	moor	moors	moored	mooring
15.	boor	boors	a Moor	Thomas Moore
16.	* **four**	fours	fourth	4th
17.	two-by-four	2x4	downpour	pouring
18.	* **pour**	pours	poured	outpouring
19.	* **your**	yours	yourself	yourselves
20.	* **or**	* for	forever	!! senor
21.	abhor	abhors	abhorred	abhorring
22.	decor	condor	picador	toreador
23.	Labrador	matador	cuspidor	corridor
24.	metaphor	ambassador	!! *por favor*	nor
25.	Thor	San Salvador	!! *signor*	unasked-for

* Homophones:

or/ore/oar	A paddle is a type of oar. Steel is made from iron ore. Believe it or not.
your/yore/you're	Your story was based on the days of yore. You're kidding, aren't you?
four/fore/for	The four boys yelled, "Fore" just for kicks.
poor/pour/pore	In some dialects, the poor say pour me a drink. If a pore gets clogged you can get a pimple.

!! "Foreign" Words:

señor ("say'n YOH'r"), Spanish for mister or sir; signor ("see'n YOH'r"), Italian for mister or sir.
por favor ("POH'r fuh VOH'r"), Spanish for please.

See the complete -ush family on p. 211 in *The Patterns of English Spelling* (TPES);
the -oor, p. 532; the -our, p. 532; the -or, p. 516.

28

	45th day	46th day	47th day	48th day
1.	* (**) our	ours	ourselves	although
2.	hour	hours	through	though
3.	* flour	* flours	thorough	thoroughly
4.	sour	sours	soured	souring
5.	scour	scours	scoured	scouring
6.	devour	devours	devoured	devouring
7.	flower	* flowers	flowered	flowering
8.	power	powers	powered	powering
9.	overpower	overpowers	overpowered	overpowering
10.	tower	towers	towered	towering
11.	shower	showers	showered	showering
12.	horn	horns	horned	horning
13.	corn	corns	corny	corniest
14.	scorn	scorns	scorned	scorning
15.	adorn	adorns	adorned	adorning
16.	* morn	* morning	morn	* morning
17.	* mourn	mourns	mourned	* mourning
18.	*** warn	warns	warned	warning
19.	acorn	acorns	popcorn	freeborn
20.	inborn	shorn	tinhorn	outworn
21.	shopworn	well-worn	forlorn	unicorn
22.	unborn	newborn	thorn	torn
23.	born	weatherworn	although	through
24.	beauty	beauties	beautiful	beautifully
25.	beautify	beautifies	beautified	beautifying

* Homophones:

our/are	You are in our house. (Midwestern American Dialect and other dialects)
our/hour	In one hour we can be in our house. (Standard dialects)
flower/flour	A bread of roses would be made from flower flour.
morning/mourning	What do you call crying early in the day? Morning mourning.

*** Apparent Exception. See p. 502 in *The Patterns of English Spelling* for the W- and -R controls and their WAR over the letter A.

See the complete -our family on p. 532 in *The Patterns of English Spelling* (TPES); the -ower, p. 532; the -orn, pp. 517.

	49th day	50th day	51st day	52nd day
1.	**port**	ports	portable	Portage
2.	import	imports	imported	importing
3.	export	exports	exported	exporting
4.	transport	transports	transported	transportation
5.	**report**	reports	reported	reporters
6.	deport	deported	deporting	deportation
7.	**support**	supports	supported	supportive
8.	sort	sorts	sorted	sorting
9.	**short**	shorts	shortage	shortages
10.	snort	snorts	snorted	snorting
11.	**sport**	sports	sportswear	life-support
12.	passport	passports	**although**	extorting
13.	extort	extorts	extorted	extortion
14.	abort	aborts	aborted	abortion
15.	escort	escorts	escorted	escorting
16.	*** fort**	forts	carport	davenport
17.	distort	distorts	distorted	distortion
18.	shortcake	shortsighted	shortcut	shortbread
19.	noun	nouns	announce	announcer
20.	pronoun	pronouns	pronounce	pronounced
21.	**count**	counts	counted	counting
22.	account	accounts	accounted	accounting
23.	**amount**	amounts	amounted	amounting
24.	**discount**	discounts	discounted	**county**
25.	mount	dismount	**mountain**	counties

* Homophones:

fort/forte   What do you call a defensive specialty? A fort forte.

See the complete -ort family on p. 519 in *The Patterns of English Spelling* (TPES); the -oun, p. 421; the -ounce, p. 257; the -ount, p. 252.

	53rd day	54th day	55th day	56th day
1.	**ounce**	ounces	bouncer	bouncers
2.	**bounce**	bounces	bounced	bouncing
3.	pounce	pounces	pounced	pouncing
4.	trounce	trounces	trounced	trouncing
5.	flounce	flounces	flounced	flouncing
6.	announce	announcing	announcer	**although**
7.	pronounce	pronouncing	pronounced	*** pronunciation
8.	mispronounce	mispronounced	mispronounced	*** mispronunciation
9.	denounce	denounced	denouncing	*** denunciation
10.	renounce	renounced	renouncing	*** renunciation
11.	**down**	**downs**	downed	downing
12.	crown	crowns	crowned	crowning
13.	**frown**	frowns	frowned	frowning
14.	**brown**	browns	brownie	brownies
15.	**drown**	drowns	drowned	drowning
16.	**clown**	clowns	clowned	clowning
17.	**town**	**towns**	downtown	township
18.	sundown	knockdown	spelldown	touchdowns
19.	touchdown	upside down	letdown	showdown
20.	**rich**	riches	richer	richest
21.	richly	** Richard	**which**	**which**
22.	**sandwich**	sandwiches	sandwiched	sandwiching
23.	**mile**	miles	miler	mileage
24.	**smile**	smiles	smiled	**smiling**
25.	**pile**	piles	piled	piling

** Heteronyms:

Richard ("RICH ur'd")/ Richard ("ree SHAH'r-d")   Many English-speaking people are descended from the French. Consequently, names may either keep the French pronunciation or take on an English pronunciation. When the name Richard is a last name coupled with a common French name such as Pierre, Maurice ("moh'r REE'ss"), etc., it is usually pronounced "ree SHAH'r-d." In Parisian French the ending /d/ is dropped.

See the complete -ounce family on p. 257 in *The Patterns of English Spelling* (TPES); the -own, p. 421; the -ich, 203; the -ile, p. 330.

	57th day	58th day	59th day	60th day
1.	**while**	awhile	**meanwhile**	worthwhile
2.	**file**	files	filed	**filing**
3.	compile	compiles	compiling	compilation
4.	unpile	unpiles	unpiled	unpiling
5.	defile	defiles	defiled	defiling
6.	stockpile	stockpiles	stockpiled	stockpiling
7.	reconcile	reconciles	reconciled	reconciliation
8.	**tile**	tiles	tiled	tiling
9.	rile	riles	riled	Riley
10.	exile	exiles	exiled	exiling
11.	* **style**	styles	styled	styling
12.	* **stile**	stiles	turnstile	turnstiles
13.	crocodile	profile	high profile	low profile
14.	lifestyle	lifestyles	senile	juvenile
15.	reptile	projectile	vile	wile
16.	* **hole**	holes	holed	holing
17.	* **whole**	wholesale	* **wholly**	* **holy**
18.	* **pole**	poles	poled	poling
19.	one ** **console**	two ** **consoles**	foxhole	posthole
20.	** **console**	consoles	consoled	consoling
21.	parole	dole	doled	consolation
22.	pigeonhole	pigeonholes	pigeonholed	pigeonholing
23.	keyhole	mole	oriole	loophole
24.	porthole	tadpole	mink stole	* **sole**
25.	* **role**	roles	casserole	insole

* Homophones:

sole/soul — What do you call an only spirit or a ghost of a shoe? A sole soul.
pole/poll — What do you call a Polish questionaire? A Pole poll.
role/roll — What do you call a part in a play for a Danish pastry? A roll role.
whole/hole — What do you call the entire empty space a digger makes? The whole hole.
wholly/holy — What do you call something completely sacred? Wholly holy.
style/stile — What do you call the latest fashion in special gates? Stile style.

** Heteronyms:
console ("KAH'n soh'l")/console ("kun SOH'l")
See the complete -ile family on p. 330 in *The Patterns of English Spelling* (TPES);
the -ole, p. 331.

32

	61st day	62nd day	63rd day	64th day
1.	* mind	minds	minded	minding
2.	* remind	reminds	reminded	reminding
3.	reminder	reminders	mastermind	masterminded
4.	bind	binds	bound	binding
5.	grind	grinds	ground	grinding
6.	blind	blinds	blinded	blinding
7.	kind	kinds	kinder	kindest
8.	** wind	** winds	** wound	winding
9.	rewind	rewinds	rewound	rewinding
10.	mankind	hind	hindsight	hindquarter
11.	mind-set	mindful	simple-minded	open-minded
12.	narrow-minded	feeble-minded	absent-minded	evil-minded
13.	** wind	** winds	windy	windiest
14.	rescind	rescinds	rescinded	rescinding
15.	cinder	cinders	Cinder Ella	Cinderella
16.	whirlwind	woodwind	tailwind	downwind
17.	upwind	headwind	windmill	windfall
18.	window	windshield	windbag	windbreak
19.	It's too bad.	It's too hot.	although	though
20.	boo	* boos	booed	booing
21.	taboo	taboos	bamboo	peek-a-boo
22.	tattoo	tattoos	tattooed	tattooing
23.	shampoo	shampoos	shampooed	shampooing
24.	woo	woos	wooed	wooing
25.	* shoo	* shoos	* shooed	* shooing

* Homophones:

mined/mind	What do you call an intellect that has been tapped? A mined mind.
remined/remind	Remind me to have that old gold mine of mine remined.
boos/booze	What do you call beverages that bring jeers instead of cheers? Boos booze.
shoo/shoe	What do you call footgear that is thrown at a cat? A shoo shoe.

** Heteronyms:

wind ("WIN'd")/wind ("WYH'n-d") It's hard for a pitcher to wind up with the wind in his face.
wound ("WOW'n-d")/wound ("WOO'n-d") He wound up his watch. His war wound hurt.

See the complete -iece family on p. 432 in *The Patterns of English Spelling* (TPES);
the -eace, p. 432; the -ead, p. 402; the -oice, p. 433; -oid, p. 403; -oil, 415.

	65th day	66th day	67th day	68th day
1.	**canoe**	canoes	canoed	canoeing
2.	* **shoe**	shoes	shoed	shoeing
3.	horseshoe	horseshoes	soft-shoe	snowshoes
4.	shoebox	shoeshine	shoetree	shoelaces
5.	**moon**	moons	honeymoon	honeymoons
6.	**spoon**	spoons	spooned	spooning
7.	**balloon**	balloons	ballooned	ballooning
8.	harpoon	harpoons	harpooned	harpooning
9.	lampoon	lampoons	baboon	baboons
10.	platoon	platoons	cartooned	cartooning
11.	maroon	maroons	marooned	raccoon
12.	**cartoon**	cartoons	cartoonist	cartoonists
13.	swoon	swoons	swooned	swooning
14.	saloon	saloons	teaspoon	tablespoon
15.	buffoon	monsoon	pontoon	spittoon
16.	cocoon	typhoon	tycoon	**loon**
17.	moonlight	moonlighting	forenoon	afternoon
18.	**boot**	boots	booted	booting
19.	**shoot**	shoots	shot	shooting
20.	shooter	* **booty**	coot	* **cootie** (cooty)
21.	hoot	* **bootie**	booties	**cooties**
22.	** **root**	roots	rooted	rooting
23.	scoot	scoots	scooted	scooter
24.	troubleshoot	troubleshooting	troubleshooter	outshoot
25.	galoot	in cahoots	shootout	a moot point

* Homophones:

shoe/shoo	What do you call footgear thrown at an animal? A shoo shoe.
booty/bootie	What do you call a bonanza of baby shoes? Bootie booty.
cooty/cootie	You have your choice of spellings: cooty or cootie.

** Heteronyms:

root "ROO't"/ root "RuuT"   In some dialects, the word root rhymes with boot and in others in rhymes with foot.

See the complete -oe family on p. 313 in *The Patterns of English Spelling* (TPES); the -oon, p. 422; the -oot, p. 429.

	69th day	70th day	71st day	72nd day
1.	**foot**	**feet**	footed	**footing**
2.	pussyfoot	pussyfoots	pussyfooted	pussyfooting
3.	underfoot	surefooted	afoot	surefooted
4.	barefoot	bare feet	barefooted	flatfooted
5.	football	footwork	footfall	footrest
6.	soot	sooty	lead-footed	**though**
7.	chamber	chambers	chambered	**although**
8.	ember	embers	**although**	* **throughout**
9.	December	December's weather	**thoroughly**	* **through**
10.	**member**	members	membership	thoroughness
11.	**remember**	**remembers**	**remembered**	**remembering**
12.	limber	limbers	limbered	limbering
13.	* timber	timbers	timberland	timberline
14.	encumber	encumbers	encumbered	encumbering
15.	cucumber	cucumbers	! bomber	! bombers
16.	**number**	**numbers**	numbered	numbering
17.	outnumber	outnumbers	outnumbered	outnumbering
18.	! beachcomber	! beachcombers	! climber	climbers
19.	humble	humbles	humbled	humbling
20.	tumble	tumbles	tumbling	tumblers
21.	rough-and-tumble	stumble	stumbled	stumbling
22.	jumble	fumbled	fumbling	jumbled
23.	mumble	mumbles	mumbled	mumbling
24.	rumble	rumbles	rumbled	rumbling
25.	grumble	grumbles	grumbled	grumbling

* Homophones:

timber/timbre   What do you call a wooden voice? Timber timbre.
throughout/threw out   Throughout the game, the umpire threw out new baseballs.

! Dumb (Silent & Stupid): *climber, bomber,* and *beachcomber* all have a silent and stupid letter b. See p. 958 in *The Patterns of English Spelling* for more examples of this pattern.

See the complete -mber family on p. 639 in *The Patterns of English Spelling*; the -umble, p. 606.

	73rd day	74th day	75th day	76th day
1.	fund	funds	funded	funding
2.	refund	refunds	refunded	refunding
3.	**under**	underage	underarm	underdog
4.	thunder	thunders	thundered	thundering
5.	blunder	blunders	blundered	blundering
6.	plunder	plunders	plundering	plundered
7.	**understand**	misunderstand	**misunderstanding**	misunderstood
8.	thunderstorm	thunderhead	thunderbolt	underwent
9.	bundle	bundles	bundled	bundling
10.	trundle	trundles	trundled	trundling
11.	**handle**	handles	handled	**handling**
12.	mishandle	mishandles	mishandled	handlers
13.	candle	candles	dandle	dandling
14.	fondle	fondles	fondled	fondling
15.	dwindle	dwindles	dwindled	dwindling
16.	swindle	swindled	swindling	swindlers
17.	kindle	kindled	kindles	kindling
18.	rekindle	rekindles	rekindled	rekindling
19.	**hunt**	hunts	hunting	hunters
20.	bunt	bunted	bunting	bluntly
21.	blunt	blunts	blunted	runts
22.	grunt	grunts	grunted	grunting
23.	stunt	stunts	manhunt	headhunter
24.	**front**	storefronts	frontage	confrontation
25.	confront	affronted	forefront	confronting

NOTE: In English spelling there is a common reversal in sounds. What should be -*del* (as it is in the name Han*del*) is spelled -*dle*. The ending pattern -*le* is extremely common as in pick*le* despite the fact that it really should be -el as in nick*el*.

See the complete -nder family on p. 642 in *The Patterns of English Spelling* (TPES); the -ndle, p. 607; the -unt, p. 249.

	77th day	78th day	79th day	80th day
1.	**ask**	asks	asked	asking
2.	mask	masks	masked	masking
3.	unmask	unmasks	unmasked	unmasking
4.	**task**	tasks	**basket**	baskets
5.	cask	casks	casket	caskets
6.	flask	flasks	gaskets	basketball
7.	* **bask**	* **basks**	basked	basking
8.	**desk**	desks	news desk	pesky
9.	**risk**	risks	risked	**risky**
10.	frisk	frisks	frisked	frisky
11.	whisk	whisks	whisked	* **whisky**
12.	whisker	whiskers	whisking	* **whiskey**
13.	* **disk**	* **disks**	* **disc**	* **discs**
14.	husk	husks	husked	husky
15.	musk	dusk	tusk	tusks
16.	Dean Rusk	* **brusk**	musky	a corn husker
17.	ranch	ranches	rancher	ranchers
18.	branch	branches	branched	branching
19.	blanch	blanches	blanched	blanching
20.	Blanch	Blanch's ranch	**thoroughly**	**although**
21.	launch	launches	launched	launching
22.	paunch	paunches	paunchy	rocket launchers
23.	haunch	haunches	staunch	raunch
24.	**!! tsk, tsk**	**tsk, tsk**	**psst!**	**psst!**
25.	beauty	beautifully	beautifying	beauties

* Homophones:

bask/Basque	To bask in the sun is enjoyable. Do you have a Basque beret?
whisky/whiskey	Some people drink whisky. Others drink whiskey.
disk/disc	Do you have the word disc on your floppy disk?
brusk/brusque	Writers generally prefer the fancy brusque to brusk.

NOTE: Please do NOT rhyme *tsk* with *whisk*. There is a reason why there is no vowel in this word. This word is the sound you make to show disapproval by placing your tongue against your front teeth and making a clicking sound. *Psst* also has no vowel. *Psst* is the sound you make to get somebody's attention when you don't want others to know you're doing it.

See the complete -sk family on p. 271 in (TPES); the -nch, pp. 206-207.

Evaluation Test #2

(After 80 Days)

#	Sentence	Pattern being tested	Lesson word is in
1.	Did your neighbor sell his pr**operty**?	operty	36
2.	The little kids spl**ashed** around in the pool all day.	ashed	39
3.	We were simply cr**ushed** to find we weren't invited.	ushed	39
4.	The thief was caught hiding in the b**ushes**.	ushes	42
5.	You can make paste by mixing fl**our** with water.	our	45
6.	Do the rains in April bring on the fl**owers** in May?	owers	46
7.	Oh, how I hate to get up in the m**orning**.	orning	48
8.	We rep**orted** the accident to the police.	orted	51
9.	Sometimes names are hard to pron**ounce**.	ounce	51
10.	My sister is taking up acc**ounting** in college.	ounting	52
11.	I wish you would stop cl**owning** around.	owning	56
12.	I wonder what the Mona Lisa was sm**iling** about.	iling	56
13.	Would you like a rept**ile** for a pet?	ile	57
14.	We won a cons**olation** prize.	olation	60
15.	I sometimes have to be rem**inded** about the time.	inded	63
16.	Would somebody please open that w**indow** for me?	indow	61
17.	Have you ever fished with a bamb**oo** pole?	oo	63
18.	It's no fun to be mar**ooned** on a desert island.	ooned	67
19.	How would you like to be rem**embered**?	embered	71
20.	I wish they would stop gr**umbling** all the time.	umbling	72

Name_____ Date_____

Evaluation Test #2

Please, please, please do NOT start until your teacher gives you the directions.
You must stay with your teacher as she reads the sentences.
All you have to do is to fill in the blanks with the missing letters.

1. Did your neighbor sell his pr_____?

2. The little kids spl_____ around in the pool all day.

3. We were simply cr_____ to find we weren't invited.

4. The thief was caught hiding in the b_____.

5. You can make paste by mixing fl_____ with water.

6. Do the rains in April bring on the fl_____ in May?

7. Oh, how I hate to get up in the m_____.

8. We rep_____ the accident to the police.

9. Sometimes names are hard to pron_____.

10. My sister is taking up acc_____ in college.

11. I wish you would stop cl_____ around.

12. I wonder what the Mona Lisa was sm_____ about.

13. Would you like a rept_____ for a pet?

14. We won a consol_____ prize.

15. I sometimes have to be rem_____ about the time.

16. Would somebody please open that w_____ for me?

17. Have you ever fished with a bamb_____ pole?

18. It's no fun to be mar_____ on a desert island.

19. How would you like to be rem_____?

20. I wish they would stop gr_____ all the time.

	81st day	82nd day	83rd day	84th day
1.	**bench**	benches	benched	benching
2.	**wrench**	wrenches	wrenched	wrenching
3.	clench	clenches	clenched	clenching
4.	stench	drench	**drenched**	thirst quencher
5.	quench	**quenches**	quenched	quenching
6.	trench	trenches	* **entrenched**	* **entrenching**
7.	* entrench	stench	* **intrenched**	* **intrenching**
8.	**inch**	inches	inched	inching
9.	**pinch**	pinches	pinched	pinching
10.	* **lynch**	lynches	lynched	lynching
11.	clinch	clinches	clinched	clinching
12.	finch	finches	pinchers	clinchers
13.	flinch	flinches	flinched	flinching
14.	cinch	cinches	cinched	cinching
15.	winch	winches	winched	winching
16.	The Grinch	The Grinch's heart	Wednesday	Wednesday
17.	**bunch**	bunches	bunched	bunching
18.	**hunch**	hunches	hunched	hunching
19.	**punch**	punches	punched	punching
20.	**crunch**	crunches	crunched	crunching
21.	brunch	brunches	luncheon	luncheons
22.	**lunch**	lunches	lunched	lunching
23.	munch	munches	munched	munchies
24.	scrunch	scrunches	scrunched up	honeybunch
25.	* **throughout**	**thoroughly**	**although**	**though**

* Homophones:

linch/lynch   You don't have to lynch the man for spelling linch pin, lynch pin.
entrench/intrench You have your choice of spellings. Most writers prefer entrench to intrench.

See the complete -nch families on pp. 206-207 in *The Patterns of English Spelling*.

	85th day	86th day	87th day	88th day
1.	**church**	churches	The church's pastor	**honest**
2.	lurch	lurches	lurched	lurching
3.	**perch**	perches	perched	perching
4.	**attach**	attaches	attached	attaching
5.	detach	detaches	detached	detaching
6.	reattach	reattaches	reattached	reattaching
7.	attachment	attachments	detachment	detachments
8.	**match**	matches	matched	matching
9.	patch	patches	patched	patching
10.	dispatch	dispatches	dispatched	dispatchers
11.	hatch	hatches	hatched	hatchery
12.	latch	latches	latched	latching
13.	snatch	snatches	snatched	hatcheries
14.	batch	batches	thatched	Catch-22
15.	* catch	catches	catching	catchers
16.	scratch	**scratches**	scratching	Mrs. Thatcher
17.	unlatch	unlatches	unlatched	unlatching
18.	etch	etches	etched	etching
19.	* retch	retches	retched	retching
20.	stretch	stretches	stretched	stretchers
21.	* wretch	wretches	*** **wretched**	* farfetched
22.	fetch	fetches	* **far-fetched**	fetching
23.	* ketch	ketches	Wednesday's child	most Wednesdays
24.	sketch	sketches	sketched	sketching
25.	Fletch	Fletcher	Fletch's sketches	**honesty**

* Homophones:

catch/ketch — A ketch can't catch up to a speedboat.
retch/wretch — What do you call a poor urchin's vomit? Wretch retch.
far-fetched/farfetched — You have your choice. Both are correct.

*** Pronounce the adjective *wretched* ("RET chid"). The verbs ending -etched are pronounced "ETCH't."

See the complete -urch family on p. 520 in *The Patterns of English Spelling* (TPES);
the -ach & -atch, p. 201; the -etch, p. 202.

	89th day	90th day	91st day	92nd day
1.	**itch**	**itches**	itched	itching
2.	* **witch**	**witches**	a **witch's** brew	two witches' brooms
3.	switch	switches	switched	switching
4.	**pitch**	pitched	pitching	* pitchers
5.	ditch	ditches	ditched	ditching
6.	snitch	snitches	snitching	a last-ditch effort
7.	hitch	hitches	hitched	hitching
8.	twitch	twitches	twitched	twitching
9.	bewitch	bewitches	bewitched	bewitching
10.	**kitchen**	kitchens	* **which**	sandwiches
11.	**picture**	**pictures**	pictured	picturing
12.	lecture	lectures	lectured	lecturing
13.	fracture	fractures	fractured	fracturing
14.	manufacture	manufactures	manufactured	manufacturing
15.	* **maid**	maids	maiden	maidens
16.	raid	raids	raided	raiders
17.	* **braid**	braids	braided	braiding
18.	**afraid**	unpaid	repaid	unrepaid
19.	**laid**	mislaid	bridesmaid	handmaid
20.	mermaid	Medicaid	milkmaid	inlaid
21.	**aid**	aids	aided	aiding
22.	**broad**	broader	broadest	broadly
23.	broadcast	abroad	broadcaster	broadcasting
24.	broadside	broad jump	broad brim	Broadway
25.	broadcloth	**honest**	**honestly**	**honesty**

* Homophones:

maid/made	The maid made up a story.
which/witch	Which witch owns the black cat?
pitcher/picture	What do you call a Nolan Ryan photo? A pitcher picture.
braid/brayed	That girl loves to braid her hair. The donkey brayed.

See the complete -itch family on p. 203 in *The Patterns of English Spelling* (TPES);
the -cture, p. 923; the -aid, p. 401; the -broad, p. 401.

	93rd day	94th day	95th day	96th day
1.	**key**	keys	keyed up	keying
2.	monkey	monkeys	monkeyed	monkeying
3.	**money**	**honey**	turkey	turkeys
4.	volley	volleys	volleyed	volleying
5.	valley	valleys	**alley**	alleys
6.	jockey	jockeys	abbey	attorney
7.	journey	journeys	journeyed	journeying
8.	pulley	chimney	chop suey	flunkey
9.	curtsey	donkey	galley	kidney
10.	New Jersey	parsley	phooey	Sidney
11.	trolley	Oprah Winfrey	baloney	Barney
12.	**they**	* **they're**	**they've**	**they'd**
13.	* **grey**	* **greys**	* **greyed**	greying
14.	* **prey**	* **preys**	* **preyed**	praying
15.	**obey**	obeys	obeyed	obeying
16.	disobey	disobeys	disobeyed	disobeying
17.	obedient	obediently	obedience	obedience
18.	disobedient	disobediently	disobedience	disobedience
19.	survey	surveys	surveyed	surveying
20.	convey	conveys	conveyed	conveying
21.	* **hey**	whey	* **trey**	Monterey
22.	**each**	tongue	**tongue**	**tongues**
23.	beach	beaches	beached	beaching
24.	* **leach**	leaches	leached	leaching
25.	bleach	bleaches	bleached	bleachers

* Homophones:

key/quay/qui	A key fits into a lock. A quay can be next to a lough. Qui?
grey/gray	The Britisher wore grey. The American wore gray.
greys/grays/graze	What do you call it when black and white sheep eat together? Greys graze.
greyed/grayed/grade	What do you call a dingy class? A greyed grade or a grayed grade.
prey/pray	Lions prey. We pray.
preys/prays/praise	The lion preys on antelope. A religious person prays, "Praise be to God."
leach/leech	If you could leach a leech, would you?
hey/hay	What do you say to get fodder's attention? Hey, Hay.
trey/tray	What do call a serving platter for three-spots? A trey tray.

NOTE: Because we read writers who use American spellings and writers who use British spellings, AVKO chooses to present both. As a parent, you are free to choose whichever you feel is most appropriate for your children. Teach either or both. It's your choice.

See the complete -ey family on pp. 306 & 302 in TPES; the -each, p. 437.

	97th day	98th day	99th day	100th day
1.	**reach**	reaches	**reached**	reaching
2.	**teach**	teaches	**teachers**	**teaching**
3.	**preach**	preaches	preachers	**preaching**
4.	overreach	overreaches	overreached	overreaching
5.	peach	**peaches**	* **beach**	beaches
6.	impeach	impeaches	impeached	impeachment
7.	* **breach**	breaches	breached	breaching
8.	**speech**	speeches	* **beech**	beeches
9.	** (*) **breech**	! **breeches**	breeched	breeching
10.	beseech	beseeches	beseeched	beseeching
11.	screech	screeches	screeched	screeching
12.	**able**	**unable**	**ability**	inability
13.	**enable**	enables	**enabled**	enabling
14.	**disable**	**disabled**	**disability**	**abilities**
15.	**table**	tables	tabled	tabling
16.	timetable	timetables	times table	times tables
17.	turntable	turntables	sable	Ken Stabler
18.	**stable**	stables	unstable	**stability**
19.	**cable**	cables	cabled	cabling
20.	fable	fables	fabled	instability
21.	**Bible**	Bibles	**noble**	nobles
22.	ruble	rubles	ennobled	nobility
23.	bauble	bauble	foible	foibles
24.	**double**	doubles	doubled	doubling
25.	**trouble**	**troubles**	**troubled**	**troubling**

* Homophones:

beach/beech	It is possible to see a beech tree while you're at the beach.
breach/breech	You shouldn't breach a contract. A breech birth is dangerous.

* Heteronyms:

breech ("breech")/breech ("brich") The preferred pronunciation is "breech," but the correct pronunciation of breeches is always "brich iz" as in "He's too big for his breeches."

! Note: The word breeches rhymes with ditches and witches!

See the complete -each family on p. 437 in (TPES); the -eech, p. 437; -ble, p, 610.

	101st day	102nd day	103rd day	104th day
1.	**star**	stars	**starred**	**starring**
2.	**scar**	**scars**	scarred	**scarring**
3.	spar	spars	**sparred**	**sparring**
4.	disbar	disbars	disbarred	disbarring
5.	par	pars	**parred**	**parring**
6.	char	charcoal	* **charred**	charring
7.	cigar	cigars	seminar	streetcar
8.	sandbar	superstar	* **czar**	**czars**
9.	bazaar	Zanzibar	* **tsar**	**tsars**
10.	**war**	wars	* **warred**	warring
11.	* **ward**	wards	warded	warding
12.	**warm**	warms	warmed	warming
13.	swarm	swarms	swarmed	swarming
14.	* **warn**	warns	warned	warning
15.	warp	warps	warped	warping
16.	wart	warts	prewar	postwar
17.	**quart**	* **quarts**	* **quartz**	warden
18.	award	awards	awarded	awarding
19.	**reward**	rewards	rewarded	rewarding
20.	warrant	warrants	warranted	warrantee
21.	dwarf	dwarfs	dwarves	dwarfing
22.	wharf	wharfs	wharves	warriors
23.	**quarter**	quarters	quartered	quartering
24.	quarterly	quarterlies	quarrelsome	warmest
25.	forewarn	forewarns	forewarned	forewarning

*Homophones:

charred/chard	What do you call burnt greens? Charred chard.
czar/tsar	Americans generally prefer czar; the British, tsar.
quarts/quartz	Why don't they measure quartz by quarts?
warn/worn	Did you warn them that the clothes they are buying have been worn before?

Teacher Notes: The letter U in qUart, qUartz, qUarter, qUarrel, & qUarry is really the consonant W (DOUBLE U") – not a vowel. The letter Q in QU words sounds as a K; i.e, QU=KW. The W- CONTROL operates in the word "WHARF" because the sound /W/ actually follows the /H/ sound as is true in all the WH-words in which the W is sounded. That is, the WH- words are normally pronounced /HW/ or just /W/. This very regular "REVERSAL" of sounds (or dropping of the /H/ sound) is rather easy to teach children to read and spell.

See the complete -ar family on p. 501 (TPES); the -war-, p. 502.

	105th day	106th day	107th day	108th day
1.	**quarrel**	quarrels	(Am.) quarreled	(Am.) quarreling
2.	quarrelsome	it's too much	(Br.) quarrelled	(Br.) quarrelling
3.	quarry	quarries	quarried	quarrying
4.	Scotch	Scotches	hopscotch	topnotch
5.	botch	botches	botched	botching
6.	notch	notches	notched	notching
7.	blotch	blotches	crotch	crotches
8.	Dutch	Dutchman	Dutchmen	it's too bad
9.	clutch	clutches	clutched	clutching
10.	hutch	hutches	Hutch	Hutchinson
11.	crutch	crutches	**cousin**	**two cousins**
12.	**such**	**too much**	much too much	lost its collar
13.	**touch**	**touches**	touched	touching
14.	retouch	retouches	retouched	retouching
15.	untouchable	touchdown	touchy	quality
16.	Butch	Butch's car	butchery	equality
17.	butcher	butchers	butchered	butchering
18.	**watch**	**watches**	**watched**	**watching**
19.	swatch	swatches	watchman	watchmen
20.	watchdog	watcheye	watchful	watchfulness
21.	watchtower	watchword	stopwatch	watchmaker
22.	swat	swats	swatted	swatting
23.	squat	squats	squatted	squatters
24.	kumquat	kumquats	! **suave**	watertight
25.	fly **swatter**	swatters	Waterloo	watermark

Notes: The letter U in qUart, qUartz, qUarter, qUarrel, qUarry and sUave is really the consonant W (DOUBLE U") · not a vowel. The letter Q in QU words sounds as a K; i.e., QU=KW. The W- CONTROL operates in the word "WHARF" because the sound /W/ actually follows the /H/ sound as is true in all the WH- words in which the W is sounded. That is, the WH- words are normally pronounced /HW/ or just /W/. This very regular "REVERSAL" of sounds (or dropping of the /H/ sound) is rather easy to teach children to read and spell.

*** **Note:** See the wa- controlled words on p. 504 of *The Patterns of English Spelling*.

See the complete -ain family on p. 419 in *The Patterns of English Spelling* (TPES); the -ant, p. 249.

46

	109th day	110th day	111th day	112th day
1.	* road	roads	carloads	truckloads
2.	load	loads	loaded	loading
3.	reload	unloaded	overloaded	toll road
4.	railroad	crossroad	off-road	payload
5.	goad	goads	goaded	goading
6.	leap	leaps	leaping	leaper
7.	* cheap	cheaper	cheapest	cheaply
8.	reap	reaps	reaping	grim reaper
9.	heap	heaps	heaped	heaping
10.	* Greece	Greek	Greeks	Greece
11.	fleece	fleeces	fleeced	fleecing
12.	speed	speeds	speeding	speeders
13.	feed	feeding	fed	feeders
14.	bleed	bleeding	bled	bleeders
15.	* need	needs	needle	needled
16.	weeds	weedy	weeder	weeding
17.	* seed	* seeder	seedy	seeded
18.	deed	deeded	thimbleweed	milkweed
19.	breed	breeding	* bred	stockbreeding
20.	* heed	heeded	indeed	nosebleed
21.	exceed	exceeded	exceedingly	exceeds
22.	proceed	proceeds	proceedings	procedures
23.	succeed	succeeds	succeeded	success
24.	seemed	seemingly	self-esteem	* teeming
25.	deem	redeem	redeeming	redeemer

* Homophones:

road/rowed/Rhode/rode — We rowed across a river to Rhode Island and rode in a taxi on a bumpy road.
cheap/cheep — What do you call an inexpensive chirp? A cheap cheep.
Greece/grease — What does a Greek call olive oil? Greece grease.
seed/cede — What do you call to surrender a potential plant? To cede a seed.
seeder/cedar — What do you call a wooden planter? A cedar seeder.
he'd/heed — What do you call it if a man would pay attention? He'd heed.
teem/team — When rivers teem with fish, there is a team of fishermen.
bred/bread — This wheat was especially bred to be made into bread.

See the complete -oad family on p. 403 in *The Patterns of English Spelling* (TPES), -eap p. 424, -eece, p. 432, -eed p. 402, -eem, 418.

	113th day	114th day	115th day	116th day
1.	**sheet**	**sheets**	sheeting	sweetness
2.	* **meet**	**meets**	**met**	**meetings**
3.	greet	greeted	greetings	sweeteners
4.	tweet	tweets	tweeted	tweeter
5.	**sweet**	sweets	sweeten	sweetened
6.	* **feet**	skeet	* **beets**	* **parakeets**
7.	fleet	sleet	discreet	discretion
8.	sweetheart	sweet-talk	indiscreet	indiscretion
9.	* **high**	* **higher**	highest	highway
10.	**sigh**	* **sighs**	* **sighed**	sighing
11.	high school	sky-high	knee-high	nigh
12.	thigh	Captain Bligh	thighbone	heigh-ho
13.	* **right**	rights	righted	* **righting**
14.	**fight**	fighter	fighting	fighters
15.	* **sight**	sights	sighted	unsightly
16.	**light**	lights	lighted	lighting
17.	lighter	lightest	lightly	thunder and **lightning**
18.	lighten	lightens	lightened	**lightening**
19.	delight	delights	delightful	delightfully
20.	* **night**	days and nights	tightfisted	headlights
21.	* **knight**	knights	knighted	knighthood
22.	swordfight	candlelight	dogfight	bullfights
23.	**flight**	flights	flighted	millwright
24.	**frighten**	frightens	**frightened**	frightening
25.	**tighten**	tightens	**tightened**	tightening

* Homophones:

meet/meat/mete	Mr. E meet Mrs. E. We eat meat. Judges mete out punishment.
feet/feat	What do you call a great jump? A feet feat.
high/hi/hie	Hi there! Hie yourself there. High up in the sky.
higher/hire	What is higher than a kite? Would you hire someone who was?
sighed/side	He sighed, "Whose side are you on?"
sighs/size	She sighs about her size.
night/knight	What do you call a Mr. by day and Sir after six? A night knight.
sight/site/cite	A judge can cite a site for being a sight.
right/rite/write/wright	Can a Wright write a rite right?

See the complete -eet family on p. 427 in *The Patterns of English Spelling* (TPES);
the -igh, p. 308; the -ight, p. 428.

	117th day	118th day	119th day	120th day
1.	**ought**	ought to	ought not to	ought to
2.	**fought**	fought	That's too bad.	forethought
3.	**bought**	bought	thoughtful	afterthought
4.	**brought**	thoughtful	thoughtfully	thoughtfulness
5.	**thought**	**thoughts**	**laugh**	laughs
6.	wrought	overwrought	laughter	laughter
7.	* **taught**	self-taught	caught	**ghost**
8.	distraught	onslaught	**honest**	**honesty**
9.	slaughter	slaughters	slaughtered	slaughtering
10.	**daughter**	daughters	my daughter's friends	Cosby's daughterS' friends
11.	for naught	naughty	naughtier	naughtiest
12.	dreadnaught	**thoroughly**	**although**	* **throughout**
13.	* **taut**	astronaut	Juggernaut	**although**
14.	**end**	ends	ended	ending
15.	**friend**	friends	**friendly**	friendship
16.	**bend**	* **bends**	bent/bended	bending
17.	**lend**	* **lends**	**lent**	lending
18.	**send**	sends	**sent**	sending
19.	**spend**	spends	**spent**	spending
20.	fend	fends	fending	fenders
21.	defend	defended	defenders	defensive
22.	offend	offended	offenders	offensive
23.	ascend	ascended	* **ascent**	ascension
24.	descend	descended	descent	descendant
25.	condescend	condescended	condescending	condescension

* Homophones:

taught/taut	We were taught that a tight rope is taut.
ascent/a scent/a cent	What do you call cheap perfume going up? A cent a scent ascent.
bends/Ben's	What Benjamin's broom does before it breaks. Ben's bends.
lends/lens	What an eye doctor does when he rents free half a pair of glasses. Lends lens.

See the complete -aught family on p. 430 and the -end on p. 208 in *The Patterns of English Spelling*.

Evaluation Test #3
(After 120 Days)

	Sentence	Pattern being tested	Lesson word is in
1.	I hope our neighbors weren't sw**indled**.	indled	74
2.	We **asked** them to come to our house first.	asked	79
3.	They sent us several b**askets** of flowers.	askets	80
4.	They had to trim several br**anches** off the tree.	anches	78
5.	Water really qu**enches** your thirst.	enches	82
6.	Children should be taught to never play with m**atches**.	atches	86
7.	The injured player was carried out on a str**etcher**.	etcher	88
8.	If there's anything I hate, it's listening to l**ectures**.	ectures	90
9.	The player suffered a fr**acture**.	acture	89
10.	It's hard to p**icture** a president in hair curlers.	icture	89
11.	It's fun to play v**olley**ball.	olley	93
12.	You shouldn't have disob**eyed** orders.	eyed	95
13.	We watched the ball game from the bl**eachers**.	eachers	96
14.	It's time we called a scr**eeching** halt to this nonsense.	eeching	100
15.	Nitroglycerin is highly unst**able**.	able	99
16.	Everybody has all kinds of different **abilities**.	abilities	100
17.	Do you remember who st**arred** in *Gone With the Wind*?	arred	103
18.	How many times do you have to be w**arned** about that?	arned	103
19.	When I hurt my foot, I had to walk on cr**utches**.	utches	106
20.	I love to hear the piano played with a light t**ouch**.	ouch	105

Name_____ Date_____

Evaluation Test #3

Please, please, please do NOT start until your teacher gives you the directions.
You must stay with your teacher as she reads the sentences.
All you have to do is to fill in the blanks with the missing letters.

1. I hope our neighbors weren't sw_____.

2. We _____ them to come to our house first.

3. They sent us several b_____ of flowers.

4. They had to trim several br_____ off the tree.

5. Water really qu_____ your thirst.

6. Children should be taught never to play with m_____.

7. The injured player was carried out on a str_____.

8. If there's anything I hate, it's listening to l_____.

9. The player suffered a fr_____.

10. It's hard to p_____ a president in hair curlers.

11. It's fun to play v_____ ball.

12. You shouldn't have disob_____ orders.

13. We watched the ball game from the bl_____.

14. It's time we called a scr_____ halt to this nonsense.

15. Nitroglycerin is highly unst_____.

16. Everybody has all kinds of different _____.

17. Do you remember who st_____ in *Gone With the Wind*?

18. How many times do you have to be w_____ about that?

19. When I hurt my foot, I had to walk on cr_____.

20. I love to hear the piano played with a light t_____.

	121st day	122nd day	123rd day	124th day
1.	befriend	befriends	befriended	befriending
2.	**blend**	blends	blending	blenders
3.	mend	*** mends**	mended	mending
4.	commend	commends	commended	commending
5.	recommend	recommended	recommending	recommendation
6.	amend	amends	amended	amendment
7.	comprehend	comprehended	comprehensive	comprehension
8.	apprehend	apprehending	apprehensive	apprehension
9.	pend	*** pends**	pended	Peter Pender
10.	**depend**	*** depends**	dependent	dependence
11.	suspend	suspends	suspending	suspension
12.	expend	expended	expending	expensive
13.	append	appended	appendix	appendage
14.	wend	wended	Wendy went Wednesday.	independence
15.	tend	*** tends**	tended	tending
16.	**attend**	attended	**two * attendants**	attention
17.	**pretend**	pretended	pretending	pretension
18.	**intend**	intended	intensive	intention
19.	contend	contended	contenders	contention
20.	extend	extended	extensive	extension
21.	overextend	overextending	overextended	overextension
22.	distend	distends	distended	distending
23.	portend	portends	portending	portent
24.	vend	vends	vending	vendors
25.	trends	dividends	legends	reverends

* Homophones:

mends/men's	A seamstress often mends men's clothing.
depends/de pens	In Brooklyn, the price of de pens depends upon their cost.
pends/pens	Who pends when a patent on pens is pending?
tends/tens	A pair of tens tends to beat most pairs.
attendants/attendance	What do you call the roll call record of helpers. Attendants' attendance.

See the complete -end family on p. 228 in *The Patterns of English Spelling* (TPES).

	125th day	126th day	127st day	128th day
1.	**any**	anyone	anybody	anywhere
2.	**anything**	any place	many	although
3.	rainy	rainier	rainiest	We're all **through**.
4.	brainy	brainier	brainiest	We're **thorough**.
5.	**tiny**	tinier	tiniest	**thoroughly**
6.	* **shiny**	shinier	shiniest	**thought**
7.	whiny	whinier	whiniest	thoughtful
8.	pony	ponies	a pony's tail	the ponies' riders
9.	**Tony**	Tony's name	Sony	Sony's sales
10.	stony	stonier	stoniest	thoughtfully
11.	* **crony**	cronies	It's too bad.	thoroughness
12.	ceremony	ceremonies	ceremonial	thoughtfulness
13.	matrimony	matrimonial	maternity	matriarchy
14.	patrimony	patrimonial	paternity	patriarchy
15.	frater	fraternal	fraternity	fraternities
16.	loony	loonies	sorority	sororities
17.	testimony	testimonial	testament	testify
18.	* **puny**	punier	puniest	Tiffany
19.	corny	cornier	corniest	Germany
20.	brawny	brawnier	brawniest	monotony
21.	mahogany	Brittany	Albany	botany
22.	monotony	destiny	destination	larceny
23.	mutiny	peony	peonies	gluttony
24.	scrutiny	felony	felonies	ebony
25.	balcony	balconies	colony	colonies

*Homophones:

shiny/shy knee	What do you call a bright leg joint that stays out of sight? A shiny shy knee.
crony/crow knee	What do you call a friend of black bird's leg joint? Crow knee crony.
puny/pew knee	What do you call a weak kneeling joint? A puny pew knee.

See the complete -ny families on pp. 717 and 718 in *The Patterns of English Spelling*.

	129th day	130th day	131st day	132nd day
1.	goof	goofed	goofy	goofiest
2.	**roof**	roofs	roofer	roofing
3.	**proof**	proofs	bulletproof	soundproof
4.	**prove**	proves	proved	**proving**
5.	hoof	hoofs	hooves	tamperproof
6.	goofproof	foolproof	waterproof	waterproofing
7.	spoof	spoofs	spoofed	spoofing
8.	*** half**	halves	halved	halving
9.	**one-half**	two loaves	sugarloaf	**laughter**
10.	**loaf**	loafs	loafed	loafing
11.	**laugh**	laughs	laughed	laughing
12.	spook	spooks	spooked	spooking
13.	kook	kooks	gadzooks	spooky
14.	**folk**	folks	*** yolk**	yolks
15.	**took**	shook	It's too hot.	It's too big.
16.	**look**	looks	looked	looking
17.	**cook**	cooks	cooked	**cookie**
18.	**book**	books	pocketbook	guidebook
19.	rook	rooks	rookie	rookies
20.	crook	crooks	crooked	cookbook
21.	brook	brooks	hook	hooked
22.	overlook	overlooked	unlooked for	partook
23.	donnybrook	jokebook	notebooks	matchbooks
24.	workbooks	scrapbook	yearbooks	passbook
25.	bookkeeper	bookkeeping	bookshelf	bookshelves

* Homophones:

yolk/yoke	What would you call an ox collar made with no egg whites? A yolk yoke.
have to/half to	To split evenly means you have to give half to the other person.

See the complete -ook family on pages 409 in *The Patterns of English Spelling*; the -olk, p. 409; the -oof, p. 407; the -ove, p. 326; the -oaf, p. 407.

	133rd day	**134th day**	**135th day**	**136th day**
1.	* **oar**	oars	oarlock	oarsmen
2.	* **soar**	soars	soared	soaring
3.	roar	roars	roared	roaring
4.	uproar	uproarious	**although**	**thoroughly**
5.	* **boar**	* **boars**	* **throughout**	thoroughness
6.	* **liar**	liars	pliers	**though**
7.	**sorry**	lorry	lorries	hurriedly
8.	**worry**	worries	worried	worrying
9.	**hurry**	hurries	hurried	hurrying
10.	scurry	scurries	scurried	scurrying
11.	flurry	flurries	It's too good.	It hurt its wing.
12.	**carry**	**carries**	**carried**	**carrying**
13.	* **marry**	**marries**	**married**	**marrying**
14.	* **ferry**	ferries	ferried	ferrying
15.	* **merry**	merrily	merriment	merry-go-round
16.	* **berry**	berries	loganberries	mulberry
17.	# cackleberry	cranberries	huckleberry	strawberries
18.	blackberry	blueberries	thimbleberry	raspberries
19.	* **fur**	furs	furrier	**honesty**
20.	purr	purrs	purred	purring
21.	spur	spurs	spurred	spurring
22.	burr	burrs	Aaron Burr	occurrence
23.	slur	slurs	slurred	slurring
24.	**occur**	occurs	**occurred**	occurring
25.	recur	recurs	recurred	recurring

* Homophones:

oar/or/ore	What do you call a choice between a paddle and metallic earth? Oar or ore.
soar/sore	To fly high is to soar. To have aches and pains is to be sore.
boar/bore	What do you call a unexciting male pig? A boar bore.
liar/lyre	What do you call a dishonest harp? A lyre liar.
fairy/ferry	What do you call a boat for magical people? A fairy ferry.
marry/merry/Mary	Would you rather marry merry Mary or wed a happy Marie?
berry/bury/Bary/Barry	Will Bary or Barry plant the fruit or bury the berry?
fir/fur	What do you call hair on an evergreen? Fir fur.

Cackleberries are eggs in several dialects.
See the complete -oar family on p. 532; -rry family on p. 706; ur family, p. 520 in *The Patterns of English Spelling*.

	137th day	138th day	139th day	140th day
1.	reoccur	reoccurs	reoccurred	reoccurring
2.	blur	blurs	blurred	blurring
3.	concur	concurs	concurred	concurrent
4.	murmur	murmurs	murmured	murmuring
5.	verb	verbs	verbal	verbally
6.	** herb	herbs	herbal	proverbs
7.	adverb	adverbs	proverb	proverbial
8.	superb	It's too big.	It's to go.	found its way
9.	* forward	forwards	forwarded	forwarding
10.	hazard	hazards	hazarded	hazardous
11.	standard	standards	nonstandard	custard
12.	* mustard	haggard	laggard	sluggard
13.	orchard	orchards	billiards	innards
14.	Spaniard	Spaniards	**! leeward	dullard
15.	windward	southward	downward	straightforward
16.	lizard	lizards	blizzard	Packard
17.	leopard	leopards	backward	homeward
18.	awkward	coward	cowards	cowardly
19.	steward	afterwards	wizard	! vineyard
20.	beard	beards	bearded	bearding
21.	Bluebeard	Blackbeard	hummingbird	mockingbird
22.	* heard	overheard	unheard of	23rd
23.	bird	birds	third	twenty-third
24.	songbird	lovebird	early bird	thirty-third
25.	blackbird	redbird	whirlybird	thirds

* Homophones:

forward/foreword   What do you call a brazen introduction? A forward foreword.
mustard/mustered   Pass the mustard, please. He was mustered out of the army.
heard/herd   Did that group of cows hear you? Yes, the herd heard me.
leeward/lured   To be lured leeward is to be coaxed to the non-windward side.

** Heteronyms:

herb ("HUR'b")/herb ("UR'b") The British pronounce the H in herb. Americans don't.
leeward ("LOO'r-d")/leeward ("LEE wurd") The nautical usage is "LOO'r-d"; landlubbers say "LEE wurd."

See the complete -ur family on p. 520 in *The Patterns of English Spelling*; wor-, p. 503;
-erb, p. 511; -ard, p. 506; -eard, p. 533; -ird, p. 514.

	141st day	142nd day	143rd day	144th day
1.	curd	curds and whey	absurd	absurdly
2.	curdle	curdles	curdled	curdling
3.	hurdle	hurdles	hurdled	hurdling
4.	hurdler	hurdlers	absurdity	absurdities
5.	Earl	Earl's stories	earl	earlier
6.	Pearl	Pearl's songs	**early**	earliest
7.	**girl**	girls	a **girl's** dress	**girls'** dresses
8.	swirl	swirls	swirled	swirling
9.	twirl	twirls	twirled	twirling
10.	whirl	whirls	whirled	whirling
11.	whirlpool	whirlwind	Shirley	Shirley's girls
12.	**firm**	firms	firmed	firming
13.	affirm	affirms	affirmed	affirmative
14.	confirm	confirms	confirmed	confirmation
15.	squirm	squirms	squirmed	squirming
16.	**form**	forms	formed	forming
17.	format	formative	formation	formations
18.	**inform**	informs	informed	**information**
19.	misinform	misinforms	misinformed	misinformation
20.	uniform	uniforms	uniformity	informative
21.	transform	transforms	transformed	transformation
22.	**perform**	performs	performed	performance
23.	conform	conforms	conformed	conformity
24.	deform	deforms	deformed	deformity
25.	norm	norms	normal	normality

See the complete -oard family on page 533 in *The Patterns of English Spelling*; -ord, p. 516; -urd, p. 520; -earl, p. 514; -irm, p. 515; -orm, p. 517.

	145th day	146th day	147th day	148th day
1.	**barn**	barns	barnyard	barnyards
2.	darn	darns	darned	darning needle
3.	**yarn**	yarns	Mr. Garner	Mrs. Garner's husband
4.	varnish	varnishes	varnished	varnishing
5.	tarnish	tarnishes	tarnished	tarnishing
6.	harness	harnesses	harnessed	harnessing
7.	* **earn**	earns	earned	**earning**
8.	**learn**	learns	learned	**learning**
9.	yearn	yearns	yearned	yearning
10.	learner	learners	earnest	earnestly
11.	**burn**	burns	burned	burning
12.	**turn**	turns	turned	turning
13.	**return**	returns	returned	returning
14.	* **urn**	urns	burner	burners
15.	spurn	spurns	spurned	spurning
16.	churn	churns	churned	churning
17.	sunburn	sunburns	sunburned	sunburning
18.	windburn	windburns	windburned	windburning
19.	turnip	turnips	harpy	harpies
20.	harp	harps	harped	harping
21.	carp	carps	carped	carping
22.	carpet	carpets	carpeted	carpeting
23.	tarp	tarps	sharpener	sharpeners
24.	**sharp**	sharps	sharpie	sharpies
25.	**sharpen**	sharpens	sharpened	sharpening

* Homophones:

earn/urn   What is another way of saying "to deserve a vase"? To earn an urn.

See the complete --earn family on page 533 in *The Patterns of English Spelling*; -urn, p. 521;
-arp, p. 502.

	149th day	150th day	151st day	152nd day
1.	warp	warps	warped	warping
2.	chirp	chirps	chirped	chirping
3.	twerp	twerps	purple	purple
4.	**first**	twenty-first	thirty-first	forty-first
5.	1st	21st	31st	41st
6.	first-born	first-class	first-hand	We're not * **through**.
7.	**thirst**	thirsts	thirsted	thirsting
8.	thirsty	thirstier	thirstiest	Martian
9.	harsh	harshly	harshness	martial law
10.	marsh	marshes	marshmallow	marshmallows
11.	* **marshal**	marshals	marshaled	marshaling
12.	Mr. * **Marshall**	Miss Marshall	marshalled	marshalling
13.	**boss**	bosses	bossed	bossing
14.	bossy	bossier	bossiest	mossy
15.	**loss**	losses	moss	mosses
16.	Ross	Ross's losses	across	glossy
17.	**cross**	crosses	crossed	crossings
18.	doublecross	doublecrosses	doublecrossed	doublecrossing
19.	gloss	glosses	glossed	glossing
20.	gross	grosses	grossed	grossing
21.	engross	engrosses	engrossed	engrossing
22.	grossly	* **grosser**	grossest	**grocery**
23.	* **grocer**	* **grocer**	grocers	**groceries**
24.	**forest**	forests	forester	forestry
25.	**interest**	**interests**	**interested**	**interesting**

* Homophones:

marshal/Marshall/martial   What do you call a militant lawman? A martial marshall.
grosser/grocer   What do you call a more vulgar food seller? A grosser grocer.

See the complete -arp family on page 508 in *The Patterns of English Spelling*; war-, p. 502;
-irp, p. 515; -irst, p. 515; -arsh, p. 509; -oss, p. 159; -est, p. 234.

	153rd day	154th day	155th day	156th day
1.	**coast**	coasts	coasted	coasting
2.	boast	boasts	boasted	boasting
3.	**roast**	roasts	roasted	roasting
4.	**toast**	toasts	toasted	toasting
5.	toaster	toasters	coaster	coasters
6.	boastful	boastfully	roaster	roasters
7.	**pity**	pities	pitied	pitying
8.	**city**	**cities**	**pitiful**	pitifully
9.	**beauty**	beauties	**beautiful**	beautifully
10.	**duty**	**duties**	dutiful	dutifully
11.	**blue**	blues	bluing	Tuesday
12.	trueblue	**Tuesday**	Tuesdays	Tuesday's child
13.	**glue**	glues	glued	gluing
14.	* **clue**	clues	clued	cluing
15.	* **clew**	clews	clewed	clewing
16.	* **flue**	flues	flu	**thorough**
17.	* **flew**	It chased its tail.	It's mine.	They're all **through**.
18.	* **flu**	It's theirs.	although	That's too much.
19.	* **influenza**	influenza	pursuit	pursuits
20.	* **sue**	sues	sued	suing
21.	pursue	pursues	pursued	pursuing
22.	**true**	truly	pursuer	pursuers
23.	* **due**	duly	dues	duly
24.	undue	unduly	truthful	truly
25.	* **dew**	truth	overdue	avenue

* Homophones:

clew/clue	The British detective looked for a clew. The American, for a clue.
flew/flu/flue	What do you call a chimney disease? The flue flu.
	What happened when the chimney exploded? The flue flew.
	What happened when the chimney disease went away? The flue flu flew away.
do/due/dew	What are you going to do when the dew is due?
influenza/In flew Enza	In flew Enza with influenza.
Sue/Sioux/Sault/Soo	Sioux City Sue knows the Soo Locks are in Sault Ste. Marie, Ontario and Michigan.

See the complete -oast family on p. 235 in *The Patterns of English Spelling* (TPES);
the -ity, p. 729; -ue, p. 314.

60

	157th day	158th day	159th day	160th day
1.	* cue	cues	cued	cuing
2.	rescue	rescues	rescued	rescuing
3.	barbecue	barbecues	rescuer	rescuers
4.	argue	argues	argued	arguing
5.	value	values	valued	valuing
6.	valuable	valuables	continuous	continuously
7.	continue	continues	continued	continuing
8.	* hue	hues	continual	continually
9.	discontinue	discontinues	discontinued	discontinuing
10.	* Hugh	Mr. Hughes	although	though
11.	* queue	queues	queued	queuing
12.	statue	statues	through	thoroughly
13.	virtue	virtues	virtuous	virtuously
14.	issue	issues	issued	issuing
15.	tissue	tissues	argument	argumentative
16.	suit	suits	suited	suiting
17.	pursuit	pursuits	suitable	suitably
18.	fruit	fruits	fruited	It's too good.
19.	body	bodies	full-bodied	You're right.
20.	anybody	somebody	nobody	everybody
21.	antibody	antibodies	student	studious
22.	study	studies	studied	studying
23.	darken	darkens	darkened	darkening
24.	blacken	blackens	blackened	blackening
25.	burden	burdens	burdened	burdening

* Homophones:

cue/Q/queue   What do you call a line formed to buy pool sticks? A cue queue.
Hugh/hue/hew   Hugh knows how to hew wood and can tell what each hue of wood means.

See the complete -ue family on p. 314 in *The Patterns of English Spelling* (TPES);
the -uit, p. 429; the -body, p. 711; -en, pp. 857-860.

Evaluation Test #4
(After 160 Days)

	Pattern Being Tested	Lesson word is in
1. What is the ch**eapest** shot you've ever heard?	eapest	111
2. We have succ**eeded** where others have failed.	eeded	111
3. The lemonade needs some extra sw**eetening**.	eetening	116
4. We were sl**ightly** late for church.	ightly	116
5. Look what the cat br**ought** in! A dead mouse!	ought	117
6. Both my d**aughters** are married and have careers.	aughters	118
7. Sometimes you need recomm**endations** to get a job.	endations	124
8. Diamond rings can be very, very exp**ensive**.	ensive	124
9. I wish you would stop pret**ending** to be an expert.	ending	123
10. What was Juliet doing up on the balc**ony**?	ony	125
11. Nobody likes to be overl**ooked**.	ooked	130
12. We were **worried** about you.	orried	135
13. Has it ever occ**urred** to you that you might be wrong?	urred	135
14. Smoking is haz**ardous** to your health.	ardous	140
15. I think you need some more inf**ormation** before you go.	ormation	144
16. I wish you would stop squ**irming** in your seat.	irming	144
17. I hope you have l**earned** your lesson.	earned	147
18. Nothing quenches your th**irst** like water.	irst	149
19. Jack is always b**oasting** about how good he is.	oasting	156
20. This test will be contin**ued** tomorrow. Just kidding.	ued	159

Name_____ Date_____

Evaluation Test #4

Please, please, please do NOT start until your teacher gives you the directions.
You must stay with your teacher as she reads the sentences.
All you have to do is to fill in the blanks with the missing letters.

1. What is the ch_____ shot you've ever heard?

2. We have succ_____ where others have failed.

3. The lemonade needs some extra sw_____.

4. We were sl_____ late for church.

5. Look what the cat br_____ in! A dead mouse.

6. Both my d_____ are married and have careers.

7. Sometimes you need recomm_____ to get a job.

8. Diamond rings can be very, very exp_____.

9. I wish you would stop pret_____ to be an expert.

10. What was Juliet doing up on the balc_____?

11. Nobody likes to be overl_____.

12. We were _____ about you.

13. Has it ever occ_____ to you that you might be wrong?

14. Smoking is haz_____ to your health.

15. I think you need some more inf_____ before you go.

16. I wish you would stop squ_____ in your seat.

17. I hope you have l_____ your lesson.

18. Nothing quenches your th_____ like water.

19. Jack is always b_____ about how good he is.

20. This test will be contin_____ tomorrow. Just kidding.

	161st day	162nd day	163rd day	164th day
1.	sadden	saddens	saddened	saddening
2.	madden	maddens	maddened	maddening
3.	thicken	thickens	thickened	thickening
4.	**open**	**opens**	**opened**	**opening**
5.	**happen**	**happens**	**happened**	**happening**
6.	sicken	sickens	sickened	sickening
7.	**loosen**	loosens	**loosened**	loosening
8.	**tighten**	tightens	**tightened**	tightening
9.	threaten	threatens	**threatened**	**threatening**
10.	**listen**	**listens**	**listened**	**listening**
12.	**fasten**	fastens	**fastened**	fastening
13.	fastener	fasteners	brightener	brighteners
14.	brighten	brightens	brightened	brightening
15.	sweeten	sweetens	sweetened	sweetening
16.	listener	listeners	sweetener	sweeteners
17.	moisten	moistens	moistened	moistening
18.	fatten	fattens	fattened	fattening
19.	christen	christens	christened	christening
20.	glisten	glistens	glistened	glistening
21.	**soften**	softens	softened	softening
22.	softener	softeners	worse	worst
23.	**straighten**	straightens	straightened	straightening
24.	worse	worst	lightning bug	bolt of lightning
25.	lighten	lightens	lightened	lightening

See the complete -en family on pp. 857-860 in *The Patterns of English Spelling* (TPES).

	165th day	166th day	167th day	168th day
1.	picket	pickets	picketed	picketing
2.	**ticket**	tickets	ticketed	ticketing
3.	**pocket**	pockets	pocketed	pocketing
4.	**rocket**	rockets	rocketed	rocketing
5.	cricket	crickets	thicket	thickets
6.	socket	sockets	bucket	buckets
7.	**jacket**	jackets	sprocket	sprockets
8.	**blanket**	blankets	blanketed	blanketing
9.	**market**	markets	marketed	marketing
10.	trinket	trinkets	junket	junkets
11.	**basket**	baskets	casket	caskets
12.	gasket	gaskets	brisket	We're not through.
13.	* **racket**	rackets	racketeer	racketeers
14.	bracket	brackets	packet	packets
15.	**target**	targets	targeted	targeting
16.	**budget**	budgets	budgeted	budgeting
17.	fidget	fidgets	fidgeted	fidgeting
18.	midget	midgets	fussbudget	fussbudgets
19.	wind can ** **buffet**	the wind buffets	we were buffeted	buffeting
20.	a ** **buffet** dinner	buffet style	open buffet	tasty buffet
21.	**diet**	diets	dieted	dieting
22.	**quiet**	quiets	quieted	quieting
23.	**quietly**	tablet	tablets	goblet
24.	toilet	toilets	toiletries	poems
25.	**poet**	poets	**poetry**	poetic

* Homophones:

racket/racquet   What do you call the making of tennis equipment? The racquet racket.

* Heteronyms:

buffet ("buh FAY") / buffet ("BUF it")   You can go to a buffet dinner. The wind can buffet you.

See the complete -et family on p. 685 in *The Patterns of English Spelling* (TPES).

	169th day	170th day	171st day	172nd day
1.	anklet	anklets	skillet	skillets
2.	booklet	booklets	wallet	wallets
3.	bullet	bullets	Hamlet	hamlets
4.	violet	violets	couplet	couplets
5.	comet	comets	bonnet	bonnets
6.	**planet**	planets	planetary	planetarium
7.	muppet	muppets	puppet	puppets
8.	**carpet**	carpets	trumpet	trumpets
9.	interpret	interprets	interpreted	interpreting
10.	interpreter	interpreters	interpretation	misinterpreting
11.	**closet**	**closets**	closeted	closeting
12.	rivet	rivets	riveted	riveting
13.	covet	covets	coveted	coveting
14.	velvet	velveteen	suet	crumpets
15.	sonnet	sonnets	cabinet	cabinets
16.	* **racquet**	racquets	goblet	goblets
17.	* **racket**	rackets	turret	turrets
18.	bracelet	bracelets	triplet	triplets
19.	* **prophet**	prophets	nugget	nuggets
20.	musket	muskets	musketeer	musketeers
21.	omelet	omelets	ringlet	ringlets
22.	pamphlet	pamphlets	mallet	mallets
23.	inlet	inlets	helmet	helmets
24.	banquet	banquets	tourniquet	tourniquets
25.	garret	garrets	Margaret	Margaret's

*Homophones:

racket/racquet — What do you call the making of tennis equipment? The racquet racket.
prophet/profit — What do you call money made from predictions? Prophet profit.

See the complete -et family on p. 685 in *The Patterns of English Spelling* (TPES).

	173rd day	174th day	175th day	176th day
1.	ought	fought	bought	ought to
2.	**thought**	thoughts	thoughtful	thoughtfulness
3.	bought	brought	brought	brought
4.	brought	thoughtless	thoughtlessness	thoughtfully
5.	**though**	**thoroughly**	They're all **through.**	We're not **through.**
6.	**although**	thoroughness	**thoroughly**	thoroughness
7.	succeed	succeeds	succeeded	succeeding
8.	**success**	successes	successful	successfully
9.	profess	professor	profession	professional
10.	depress	depressed	depression	depressions
11.	**discuss**	discussed	discussing	discussions
12.	**skipping**	skipper	skipped	skips
13.	**whips**	whipped	whippings	whipping
14.	**crush**	crushed	crushing	crushes
15.	**splash**	splashed	splashing	splashes
16.	**remember**	remembers	remembered	remembering
17.	grumble	grumbled	grumbles	grumbling
18.	swindle	swindled	swindlers	swindling
19.	**branch**	branches	branched	branching
20.	**stretch**	stretched	stretchers	stretches
21.	lecture	lectures	lectured	lecturing
22.	**picture**	pictures	pictured	picturing
23.	**crutch**	crutches	warned	warnings
24.	**daughter**	two daughters	my daughter's friend	It's too hard
25.	**laughter**	laughing	laughed	laughs

See the complete -ought family on p. 117 in *The Patterns of English Spelling* (TPES);
the -ough, p. 214; the -eed, p. 402; the -ess, p. 157; -uss, p. 160;
-ip, p. 128; -ash, p. 209; -ush, p. 211; -mber, p.639; -mble, p. 606
-nch, pp. 206-207; -etch, p. 202; -cture, p. 923; utch, p. 205;
aughter, p. 430.

	177th day	178th day	179th day	180th day
1.	**preach**	preaches	preachers	preaching
2.	**double**	doubles	**doubled**	**doubling**
3.	**trouble**	troubles	**troubled**	**troubling**
4.	**award**	awards	awarded	awarding
5.	**reward**	rewarded	rewarding	rewards
6.	**dwarf**	dwarfs	dwarfed	dwarfing
7.	**touch**	touches	untouched	touching
8.	swatch	swatches	watchful	watchfulness
9.	**flight**	slightly	unsightly	lightest
10.	**defend**	defended	defending	defenders
11.	**befriend**	befriended	friendly	friendliness
12.	**rainy**	tiny	tiniest	shiny
13.	crony	cronies	corny	corniest
14.	corny	cornier	**corniest**	**proof**
15.	**prove**	proves	**proved**	**proving**
16.	**remove**	removes	**removed**	**removal**
17.	**approve**	approves	**approved**	**approval**
18.	**marry**	married	**marries**	**marrying**
19.	**hurry**	hurried	**hurries**	**hurrying**
20.	**occur**	occurs	**occurred**	**occurring**
21.	**standard**	afterwards	cowardly	hazard
22.	**confirm**	squirming	affirm	affirmative
23.	**conform**	performing	transformer	forest
24.	**sharpening**	sharpened	thirsty	interesting
25.	**continued**	continuing	barbecue	rescuers

See the complete -each family on p. 437 in *The Patterns of English Spelling* (TPES);
the -war-, p. 502; the -ight, p. 428; the -ny, p. 718-19;
-ove, p. 326; -rry, p. 706; -ur, p. 520; -ard, p. 506; -irm, p.515;
-orm, p. 517; -ue, p. 314.

FINAL EVALUATION TEST

		Pattern being tested	Lesson word is in
1.	I hope we don't have another dep**ression**.	ession	4
2.	We'll have a group disc**ussion** tomorrow.	ussion	4
3.	I love going to wedding rec**eptions**.	eptions	16
4.	We were really **worried** about you.	worried	27
5.	My cousin sk**ipped** the fourth grade.	ipped	35
6.	We were simply cr**ushed** to find we weren't invited.	ushed	39
7.	My sister is taking up acc**ounting** in college.	ounting	52
8.	I sometimes have to be rem**inded** about the time.	inded	63
9.	It's no fun to be mar**ooned** on a desert island.	ooned	67
10.	I wish they would stop gr**umbling** all the time.	umbling	72
11.	They had to trim several br**anches** off the tree.	anches	78
12.	The injured player was carried out on a str**etcher**.	etcher	88
13.	The player suffered a fr**acture**.	acture	89
14.	Do you remember who st**arred** in *Gone With the Wind*?	arred	103
15.	When I hurt my foot, I had to walk on cr**utches**.	utches	106
16.	We have succ**eeded** where others have failed.	eeded	111
17.	Both my d**aughters** are married and have careers.	aughters	118
18.	Has it ever occ**urred** to you that you might be wrong.	urred	135
19.	I hope you have l**earned** your lesson.	earned	147
20.	Jill is always b**oasting** about how good she is.	oasting	156
21.	What's h**appening**?	appening	164
22.	I wish people were better l**isteners** than talkers.	isteners	162
23.	We are on a really tight b**udget**.	udget	165
24.	My cousin plays the tr**umpet**.	umpet	171
25.	I hate being called in and put on the c**arpet**.	arpet	169

Name_____ Date_____

Final Evaluation Test

Please, please, please do NOT start until your teacher gives you the directions.
You must stay with your teacher as she reads the sentences.
All you have to do is to fill in the blanks with the missing letters.

1. I hope we don't have another depr_____.
2. We'll have a group disc_____ tomorrow.
3. I love going to wedding rec_____.
4. We were really _____ about you.
5. My cousin sk_____ the fourth grade.
6. We were simply cr_____ to find we weren't invited.
7. My sister is taking up acc_____ in college.
8. I sometimes have to be rem_____ about the time.
9. It's no fun to be mar_____ on a desert island.
10. I wish they would stop gr_____ all the time.
11. They had to trim several br_____ off the tree.
12. The injured player was carried out on a str_____.
13. The player suffered a fr_____.
14. Do you remember who st_____ in *Gone With the Wind*?
15. When I hurt my foot, I had to walk on cr_____.
16. We have succ_____ where others have failed.
17. Both my d_____ are married and have careers.
18. Has it ever occ_____ to you that you might be wrong.
19. I hope you have l_____ your lesson.
20. Jill is always b_____ about how good she is.
21. What's h_____?
22. I wish people were better l_____ than talkers.
23. We are on a real tight b_____.
24. My cousin plays the tr_____.
25. I hate being called in and put on the c_____.